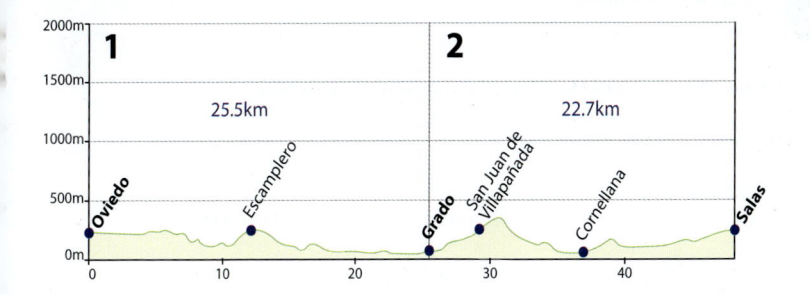

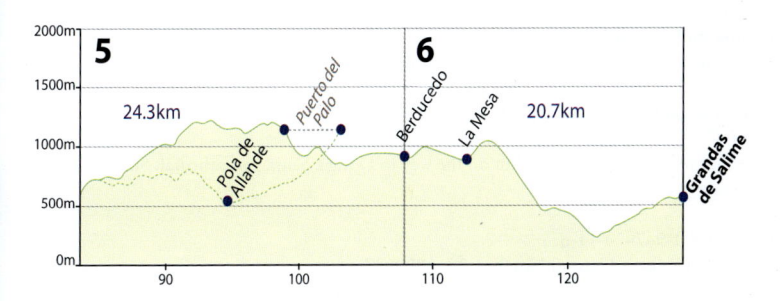

1
25.5km

Oviedo — Escamplero

2
22.7km

Grado — San Juan de Villapañada — Cornellana — Salas

5
24.3km

Pola de Allande — Puerto del Palo

6
20.7km

Berducedo — La Mesa — Grandas de Salime

9
30.2km

Vilabade — Castroverde — Lugo

10
26.1km

Lugo — San Román da Retorta — Ferreira

13
22.0km

Lavacolla — Monte de Gozo — San Marcos — Santiago

have more transportation connections, food, lodging and other services.

Camino Primitivo

Camino Primitivo: Oviedo to Santiago on Spain's Original Way
Matthew Harms, Anna Dintaman, David Landis
1st edition, January 2019

Copyright © 2018-2019 Village to Village Press, LLC
Village to Village® is a registered trademark of Village to Village Press, LLC.

Village to Village Press, LLC, Harrisonburg, VA, USA
www.villagetovillagepress.com

Photographs/Diagrams
All photographs and diagrams © Village to Village Press, LLC

Cover Photographs by Matthew Harms and David Landis
Front: Descending from Puerto del Palo
Back (left to right): Abandoned hut on the way to Doriga, Santiago Cathedral, Sunrise on mountain paths leaving Tineo

ISBN: 978-1-947474-11-6
Library of Congress Control Number: 2018909337

Text, photographs, images and diagrams © Village to Village Press, LLC, 2018-2019
Map data based on openstreetmap.org, © OpenStreetMap contributors
Cover and book design by David Landis

All rights reserved. No part of this publication may be reproduced, stored in a retrieval system or transmitted in any form or any means, digital, electronic, mechanical, photocopying, recording or otherwise, except brief extracts for the purpose of review, without the written permission of the authors.

Disclaimer*: Every reasonable effort has been made to ensure that the information contained in this book is accurate. However, no guarantee is made regarding its accuracy or completeness. Reader assumes responsibility and liability for all actions in relation to using the provided information, including if actions result in injury, death, loss or damage of personal property or other complications.*

Note about town names: We generally use the Spanish name for cities and towns, though most also have a name or spelling in the local language. We occasionally use the local language name when it is the most prominent.

Visit **caminoguidebook.com** for more information.

Contents

- **Camino Elevation Profile** 1
- **Introduction to the Route** 4
- **Travel on the Camino** 6
- **Preparing to Walk the Camino** 10
- **The Camino Primitivo** 16

Connector from Camino del Norte, 43.6km
A1: Villaviciosa to Pola de Siero, 26.9km..................................16
A2: Pola de Siero to Oviedo, 16.7km..20

Asturias, 173.0km
1: Oviedo to Grado, 25.5km...24
2: Grado to Salas, 22.7km...26
3: Salas to Tineo, 19.8km..30
4: Tineo to Borres, 15.6km..34
   4A: Tineo to Pola de Allande, 26.6km....................................36
   5A: Pola de Allande to Berducedo, 17.8km...........................37
5: Borres to Berducedo, 24.3km...38
6: Berducedo to Grandas de Salime, 20.7km..............................40

Galicia, 180.4km
7: Grandas de Salime to A Fonsagrada, 25.7km..........................42
8: A Fonsagrada to O Cádavo, 24.3km..44
9: O Cádavo to Lugo, 30.2km..46
10: Lugo to Ferreira, 26.1km..50
11: Ferreira to Melide, 21.1km...52
12: Melide to Arca, 33.0km..54
13: Arca to Santiago, 20.0km...58

- **Spanish Phrasebook** 62
- **About the Authors** 64
- **Legend** 65

Camino Primitivo

The Camino Primitivo

The Camino Primitivo, or "Original Way," is the oldest official Camino route. Today most pilgrims begin in Oviedo, but those walking the Camino del Norte can connect to the Camino Primitivo via Villaviciosa (stages A1 and A2). When thinking of the "Camino" many imagine the Francés route, traversing from St-Jean-Pied-de-Port over the Pyrenees into Spain to Santiago. In reality, there are many Caminos, echoing the ancient roads that pilgrims trod to visit the apostle's tomb.

The Camino Primitivo has rich historical significance as the oldest Camino route. As the Muslim conquest of Spain gained ground northward in the 8th century, the Kingdom of Asturias in northern Spain remained under Christian control, with its capital in Oviedo. During Alfonso II's reign in the early 9th century, St. James' remains were discovered in Galicia. Alfonso traveled to Galicia to confirm their authenticity, establishing the first Camino to Santiago. After the shift of the royal court to León and the Reconquest of Spain in the 11th century, the Camino Francés became the preferred route for pilgrims traveling to Santiago.

The Primitivo—crossing the rugged, mountainous interior of Asturias—is the most physically demanding of the modern routes to Santiago and arguably the most beautiful. Because the Primitivo has many fewer pilgrims, the route also has had fewer services than other Camino routes, though waymarking is good and services continue to improve. The upside of fewer walkers means more solitude.

INTRODUCTION TO THE ROUTE

St. James

In the New Testament, St. James is referred to as a disciple of Jesus who left his trade as a fisherman to follow Jesus. The Bible tells us little about him, save that he requested to be seated at the right hand of Jesus in heaven and was present at many important events such as the Transfiguration and Jesus weeping in the Garden of Gethsemane. The last biblical mention of James is of his martyrdom by Herod Agrippa in 44CE. St. James became known as the patron saint of Spain not from biblical account, but from tradition, oral history, legend and myth. The story goes that James preached in Iberia with little success. Mary appeared to James with the pillar to which Jesus was tied to be whipped and instructed him to build a church in Zaragoza. Shortly after his encounter with Mary, James returned to Jerusalem and was martyred, and his body was transported to Spain on a stone ship. The ship landed at Iria Flavia (present-day Padrón), and James' disciples met the ship there to move his body for burial on a nearby hill. The body was forgotten until 813CE when a Christian hermit saw a light that led him to the grave. The bishop authenticated these relics, and King Alfonso II built a chapel to the saint. The event that catapulted this modest shrine to a major pilgrimage site was the mythical Battle of Clavijo in 852, when St. James was said to have appeared to assist the Christian army against Muslim invaders. This image of St. James was a convenient motif to draw Christian support to the frontier of Christian-Muslim battle and to bolster interest and financial investment in maintaining Christian domination of Iberia. The current cathedral was begun in the year 1075 and completed in the 1120s.

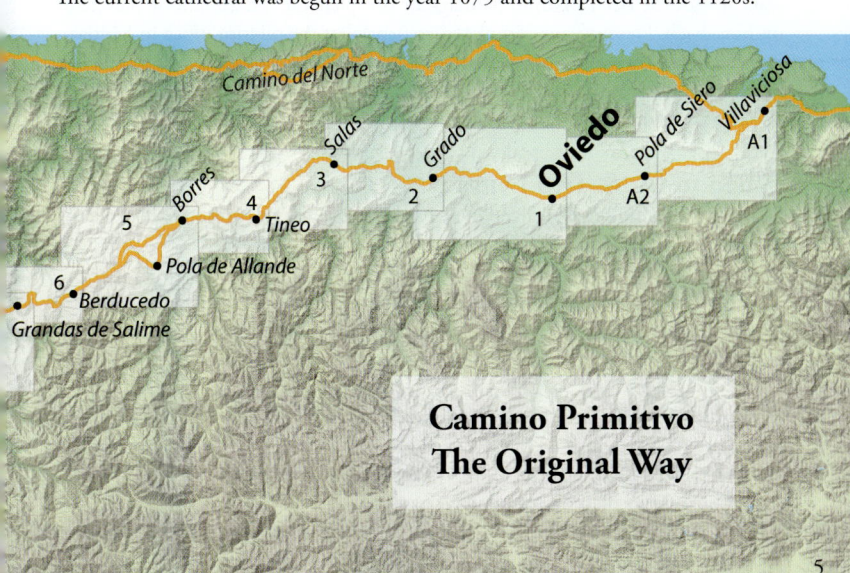

**Camino Primitivo
The Original Way**

Camino Primitivo

The Camino Experience
The Camino de Santiago is a network of historical pilgrimage routes throughout Europe that lead to Santiago de Compostela in Spain, the traditional burial place of Saint James. Rather than a remote wilderness trek, the Camino weaves through villages, towns, and even large cities. Walkers need not carry a heavy pack since frequent hostels and restaurants mean you can forego a tent, sleeping bag, and food resupply. The more popular Camino routes are well-trodden enough that you can be practically guaranteed walking companions in any season other than winter.

Many undertake the Appalachian, Pacific Crest Trail, or similar for wilderness and solitude, neither of which are primary experiences on the Camino, which offers camaraderie, encounters with culture and history, and, for many, a spiritual experience. Since the Camino routes were used for religious pilgrimage, any walker is generally considered a pilgrim, even if walking more for sport than spirituality.

Pilgrim Practicalities
The *Credencial* or "**pilgrim passport**" is a document carried by Camino walkers that allows access to pilgrim lodging and also bestows free or reduced entry to some museums and cathedrals. Collect stamps (*sellos*) at accommodations and other landmarks, which serve as proof of completing the pilgrimage to receive a *Compostela*. The ***Compostela*** is a document of completion awarded to those who walk at least the last 100km to Santiago or complete the last 200km by bicycle or on horseback. Present your completed credencial at the pilgrim office in Santiago in order to get the Compostela, written in Latin and personalized with your name and date of completion. Be sure to collect at least two stamps per day for the last 100km. Cardboard tubes are available for carrying your Compostela back home.

When to Go & Trip Length ☺
While the Camino can be walked in any season, summer and autumn are generally considered the best times for the Primitivo route.

  Spring - Cool-cold temperatures, flowers, most services open, rain likely
  ⭐**Summer** - Most popular and crowded, weather can be warm, all services open
  ⭐**Autumn** - Pleasant temperatures, most services open
  Winter - Cold and rainy with potential for snow, many services closed

How much time do I need? We recommend 2 weeks for the full itinerary. We have divided the journey into 13 daily stages from Oviedo (15 from Villaviciosa), with an average daily distance of 23.8km (14.8mi). Feel free to deviate from this pace, staying at intermediary accommodations, which are noted on maps and in the text. Many pilgrims start in Lugo (100km from Santiago) in order to qualify for a Compostela; however, starting in Lugo misses some of the best walking sections.

TRAVEL ON THE CAMINO

Visas and Entry 🔗
Spain is among the 26 Schengen states of the European Union (EU) that have no internal borders. Citizens of the USA, Canada, Australia, New Zealand, and some South American countries are issued a free visa upon arrival with valid passport, limited to 90 days within a 180-day period. Most African, Asian, Middle Eastern, and some South American nationalities must apply for an advance visa. Check EU regulations to see if your nationality requires an advance visa.

Sleeping A H ⛺ 🔗
One of the unique features of the Camino routes is the network of affordable pilgrim lodging known as *albergues.* Albergues are simple **dormitory accommodations** intended for non-motorized pilgrims (traveling on foot, by bicycle, or on horse). They are generally operated by the local municipality, parish, pilgrim confraternity, or a private owner. Many operate on a first-come first-serve basis, though most private albergues accept reservations. Lower-cost albergues often fill up quite early in the day during popular seasons. On the Primitivo route, albergues tend to be more basic and rustic (especially in Asturias) than on other routes. In Galicia, public albergues are operated by the Xunta (governing body) and have a standardized price of €6. They tend to be basic, and kitchens often lack cookware.

Costs typically range between €5-15 per person, with a few on a donation basis (*donativo*). Amenities range from very basic to all the "bells and whistles." Amenities are shown in the text through symbols (legend on inside back cover). Accommodations with their own website have a 🔗 symbol (links listed at **caminoguidebook.com**). Unless otherwise noted, assume that all albergues offer a mattress, pillow, bathroom with shower, and a place to handwash clothing. It's expected that you will bring a sleeping bag or sleep sack. The person in charge of an albergue is called a *hospitalero* (male) or *hospitalera* (female), though many public albergues have no full-time hospitalero and an attendant will come at a prearranged time to register pilgrims. In areas with fewer dedicated pilgrim services, **hotels** and **pensions** often offer special pilgrim prices.

Spain offers a wide range of accommodations for every budget. **A Hostel/Albergue** prices refer to a dormitory bed. If a hostel also has **A H private rooms**, the prices indicate dorm bed/single room/double room prices (€10/30/50). For **H hotels**, we list the single (if available)/double prices per room. Most albergues are open from around April 1 to November 1, with some staying open year round. Note that hotel prices are significantly higher in July/Aug. There are a few formal **⛺ campgrounds** on the route, but carrying a tent is uncommon as "wild camping" is not generally permitted, and reasonably priced lodging is available each night.

Camino Primitivo

Eating
Cafes and restaurants are not as readily available as on the Francés route. We list town and villages with restaurants, but in smaller towns the open hours can vary. Larger towns and cities have grocery stores, and it is wise to carry some snacks. Dinner often consists of a *Menú Peregrino* with starter, main dish, wine, bread, and dessert for around €8-12. Some lodging have a guest kitchen where you can cook your own meal. With special dietary considerations, such as gluten free, vegetarian or vegan, it may be challenging to find food that fits your needs in restaurants, especially since meat and animal products are staples of Spanish cuisine. Grocery stores in cities typically have a wide variety of foods including gluten free products, so plan ahead and carry some extra supplies.

Transportation
The closest airport to Oviedo is the Asturias Airport (regular bus service to Oviedo). Oviedo is also accessible by train. Common connecting cities are Madrid, Barcelona, London, and Paris. Some of the towns on the Primitivo route are along the Renfe FEVE narrow gauge **railway line**, but because of the mountains, much of the route is inaccessible by train. Many of the smaller towns have infrequent bus service, although there are a number of taxi services along the Primitivo. Hitchhikers are rarely picked up and should assume all known risks. Towns and cities with daily transport access are labeled with respective symbols in stage chapters.

Money, Costs and Budgeting
The unit of **currency** in Spain is the euro, made up of 100 euro cents. The best way to obtain euros is to use ATM/cash machines, available in cities and many towns marked in text with € symbol. Pilgrim hostels and small town amenities work on a cash basis, but some hotels, restaurants, and shops accept credit cards. **Daily costs** for many pilgrims are simply lodging, food/drink, and sometimes incidentals like first aid supplies, laundromat or luggage transfer. An average daily budget probably falls in the €30-50 range, depending on your frugality, though it may be possible to spend a bit less and definitely to spend a lot more, particularly if you prefer hotels to hostels. Currency: US $1 ≈ EU €0.81, EU €1 ≈ US $1.23, EU €1 ≈ UK £0.8

Bed Bugs, a blood-sucking parasitic insect, are on the rise around the world and can be a minor problem along the Camino. While bed bugs do not carry any known diseases, bites can be very uncomfortable and cause painful rashes for some people, and they are very difficult to get rid of once infested. You can pretreat your sleeping bag and backpack with permethrin and check that any albergue you stay in has been fumigated recently to lower your chances of being bitten.

TRAVEL ON THE CAMINO

Phones and Internet

You can enable international roaming on your home mobile phone plan or purchase a Spanish SIM card (which requires an unlocked phone). International roaming on many US and Canada based plans can be quite expensive, but is a good solution if only used for emergencies. T-Mobile has free international data and text on some US plans. Calling and messaging apps like WhatsApp, Viber, or Skype can be used when you have a wifi connection if you choose not to have cellular data coverage.

- To call Spain (+34) from the USA: 011 - 34 - XXX-XXXX
- To call the USA and Canada (+1) from abroad: 00 - 1 - XXX-XXX-XXXX

Wifi ("wee-fee") is increasingly available along the route; many accommodations and cafés offer free access. Some lodgings still have **desktop computers** for guest use while larger cities may have internet cafés.

Luggage Transfer and Tours

The Post Office (Correos) provides bag transfer between Oviedo to Santiago for a flat fee of €52. Weight (<20kg) and distance (<25km/90km on bike) restrictions apply. Book online, or call or WhatsApp 683440022. Taxi Camino also offers baggage transfer between Oviedo and Lugo 619156730. Note that some public albergues don't accept walkers who use transfer services.

Medical Care

Spain has good medical care that is free for citizens and countries with reciprocal agreements. Citizens of Great Britain, Ireland, and the EU need a European Health Insurance Certificate (EHIC). Non-EU citizens are recommended to have private health and travel insurance. Carry an emergency contact card with known allergies, pertinent medical history, and information that is helpful to medical staff if you are unable to communicate. In emergencies, dial 112 to reach emergency services. Pharmacies are well stocked and readily available in cities and larger towns.

Safety Issues

Spain has very low crime rates, and violent crime is extremely rare. It is always good to remain aware of your surroundings, not leave valuables unattended, and report any incidents to the police by dialing 112. Be extremely careful when walking along roads– always walk on the left side opposite traffic and remain alert. Try to avoid walking after dark. Aggressive **dogs** are not common but may be encountered. Carrying a walking stick can enhance confidence when encountering animals. All dogs in Spain are required to be vaccinated against rabies.

More planning info at **caminoguidebook.com** and **caminocyclist.com**.

Packing for the Road: Gear, Resupply and Navigation
He who would travel happily must travel light. -Antoine de Saint-Exupéry

A light load makes for a happy pilgrim, and weight should be a primary concern in packing. A popular guideline is to pack no more than 10% of your body weight. Resist the temptation to pack many extras "just in case." Shops are readily available in Spain and most anything lacking can be purchased along the way.

Backpacks: A 30-40L (1800-2500in^3) pack is sufficient for warm weather (40-60L for winter). Measure your torso length and choose a pack of the proper size, preferably being fitted at a knowledgeable outdoor retail store. Aim for a pack that weighs less than 1.4kg (3lbs) when empty.

Footwear: Light boots or sturdy trail runners with a stiff or semi-rigid sole offer protection for your feet and ankles against the often hard-surfaced, rocky, and uneven path (trail surfaces, p. 14). Get fitted for footwear in the afternoon or evening after feet have expanded during the day. Bring some kind of lightweight footwear to wear in the evenings, such as flip-flops or foam sandals. ⚠ Be sure to thoroughly break in your footwear before beginning the Camino with practice hikes wearing your loaded pack. Invest in wool socks (not cotton), which wick moisture away from your skin, dry quickly, insulate when wet, and manage odor better. If you're prone to blisters, experiment with liner socks (wool or polypropylene) to create an extra rubbing layer other than your skin.

Sleeping Bags: Most pilgrims prefer a lightweight, mummy-style, 1-season summer sleeping bag (rated $^+40+°F/^+5+°C$) for the summer season. Some opt for only a sleeping bag liner in the heat of summer. For winter and the cool edges of fall and spring, it's a good idea to have a 3-season sleeping bag (rated $^+15-^+35°F/^-10-0°C$). Buy the lightest bag you can afford within your desired temperature range.

Clothing: Consider hiking clothes as layers, with inner layers for moisture management, middle for insulation, and outer for weather protection. The general rule for outdoor clothing is to avoid cotton as it does not retain insulating properties when wet and dries slowly. Synthetic materials (polyester, nylon, spandex) and wool (especially merino) are preferred, especially in cold and wet weather. In warm seasons, choose lightweight breathable clothes that provide sun protection.

PREPARING TO WALK THE CAMINO

Be prepared for the sun with a wide-brimmed **hat** and **sunglasses,** and use **sunscreen** regularly. Bring a **lightweight rain jacket** with a waterproof breathable membrane, or use a poncho that can also cover your backpack. Bring a waterproof pack cover or line your pack with plastic garbage bags to keep your gear dry. Pack electronics in zippered plastic bags or dry bags to protect against moisture.

Hypothermia is possible in wet, cool weather (as is common on the Primitivo route), so be prepared with a dry set of clothes (socks included) for after a rainy day and bring one insulating layer, such as a warm fleece or down sweater.

Water and refills: While water is readily available most days of the Camino, it is important to carry sufficient amounts. Always carry at least one liter, and refill often. Carry more than two liters on hot days or in more remote areas. Reliable water refill sites are marked on stage maps (💧). Tap water in Spain is treated and drinkable (*potable*). Most historic springs are marked as undrinkable (*no potable*) because they have not been treated or tested. Bottled water is widely available but is less environmentally friendly than refillable bottles.

Dehydration and heat-related illness: Dehydration can lead to fatigue, headaches, heat exhaustion, and heat stroke (a dangerous and life-threatening condition). Be sure to eat foods that help to replenish electrolytes and consider an electrolyte drink, such as Aquarius™, on hot days. If you become dehydrated and overheated and are unable to cool down, take a break in a cool, shady place, rehydrate with electrolytes, and cool with a wet cloth or fanning until you feel better.

Fitness and Training: The Camino is not a technically challenging hike, but the journey's length and climbs takes a toll on the body. Taking the time to practice before beginning the pilgrimage will greatly reduce possible injuries. Training walks will help you get used to your gear, the weight on your feet and shoulders, and any other potential issues you might be able to prevent. It's wise to get used to full-day walks, taking 2-3 shorter walks per week and one full-day walk weekly with your loaded backpack. Check with your doctor if you have concerns about your health or fitness level, and start out slow and gradual.

Blister Prevention: The most common injury can cause an end to your trip.
- <u>At home</u>: choose properly fitting footwear. Try on many options before buying (foot should not move or slip when walking on various terrain types and grades). Use wool socks and liners. Break in footwear by taking hikes with a loaded pack prior to beginning the Camino.
- <u>On the trail</u>: keep feet cool and dry, take off shoes and socks for breaks, wash feet and socks daily, use liner socks.

Camino Primitivo

Packing List

Hiking Gear Essentials

- ☐ **Backpack** (30-40L)
- ☐ **Sleeping bag or bag liner**, lightweight
- ☐ **Navigation**: guidebook, GPS (optional)
- ☐ **Headlamp** or flashlight/torch
- ☐ **Sun protection**: hat, sunglasses, sunscreen and lip balm
- ☐ **Towel**, lightweight travel type
- ☐ **Water bottles** and/or **hydration system** (2L)
- ☐ **Waterproof pack cover/poncho**
- ☐ **Pocket/utility knife** (checked luggage)
- ☐ **Lighter** or **matches** (buy locally)
- ☐ **Toiletries** (list opposite)
- ☐ **Personal items** (list opposite)
- ☐ **First aid kit** (list opposite)

Take the time to visit a quality outdoor gear shop to get fitted for a backpack that is comfortable and footwear that fits properly.

Footwear & Clothing

- ☐ **Footwear** (boots or trail runners)
- ☐ **Sandals** or flip-flops
- ☐ **Hiking socks** (3 pairs wool)
- ☐ **Sock liners** (1-2 pairs wicking)
- ☐ **Pants** (1-2 pairs quick-drying, zip-offs, or shorts)
- ☐ **Short-sleeved shirts**, tank tops (1-2)
- ☐ **Long-sleeved shirts** (1-2)
- ☐ **Light fleece** or jacket
- ☐ **Waterproof jacket** or poncho
- ☐ **Underwear** (3 pairs)
- ☐ **Sports bras** (2)
- ☐ **Bandana** or Buff
- ☐ **Swimsuit** (optional)
- ☐ **Warm hat***
- ☐ **Insulating jacket***
- ☐ **Long underwear** top/bottom*

*only necessary in cold seasons

Additional Gear (Optional)

- ☐ **Hiking poles**: Used correctly, poles can take up to 25% pressure off of your leg joints. Poles are great for stability, especially going up and down hills, and serve double-duty as a means to chase away dogs. Worthwhile for anyone with joint issues. Inexpensive poles can be purchased in on route.
- ☐ **Sleeping mat**: A lightweight foam pad can come in handy for sitting on and for sleeping if albergues are full or have limited beds. You can often find left behind mats for free along the Camino.
- ☐ **Pillowcase**: Most albergues have pillows but do not change the pillowcases regularly, a spare T-shirt can also be stretched over the pillow as a makeshift case.
- ☐ **Stuff sacks** or cloth bags with drawstrings don't weigh much and keep you organized
- ☐ **Reusable nylon grocery bag**: Comes in handy as a laundry bag, purse and grocery bag
- ☐ **Clothespins** or safety pins for hanging laundry.
- ☐ **Travel cooking pot and utensils**: Many of the albergues in Galicia have kitchens, but no kitchen equipment whatsoever. If you are intent on cooking your own dinners, you may wish to bring a lightweight cooking pot, or purchase one when you arrive in Galicia.
- ☐ **Camping gear:** Lightweight tent (TarpTent) or bivy sack, camping stove, a pot and utensils, and extra water carrying capacity. (See Camping p. 7).

***For recommendations on specific brands and models, visit caminoguidebook.com.**
***Decathlon** is a chain of outdoor gear retailers throughout Spain with stores in Irún, Bilbao, Santander, Gijón, Oviedo, and Santiago de Compostela, as well as Madrid and Barcelona.

TOILETRIES
Don't pack too much. Bring small refillable travel bottles of shampoo and conditioner <100mL/4oz. Refill from items left behind (ask at the albergues) or buy your own refill and share.

- ☐ **Shampoo/conditioner** (100mL/4oz bottles)
- ☐ **Toothbrush** and **toothpaste** (travel sized)
- ☐ **Soap**, biodegradable bar or liquid, such as Dr. Bronner's™
- ☐ **Laundry detergent** (powder works well and weighs less) or 100mL/4 oz. bottle or solid bar
- ☐ **Toilet paper** or tissues (albergues frequently run out)
- ☐ **Deodorant** (optional, you will stink with or without it!)
- ☐ **Hand sanitizer** (optional)
- ☐ **Contact solution** (if necessary), replace at pharmacies

FIRST AID/MEDICAL KIT
Supplies are available in pharmacies along the route and most albergues have a basic medical kit. It's always best to be prepared with at least a few day's worth of each supply. Keep it light!

- ☐ Any **prescription medicine** you need
- ☐ Variety of **Band-Aids®/plasters, sterile gauze pads**
- ☐ Antiseptic towelettes or **wound disinfectant**
- ☐ **Antibiotic ointment**
- ☐ **Medical tape**
- ☐ **Elastic bandage** (such as ACE™)
- ☐ **Pain reliever/fever reducer** (such as acetaminophen or ibuprofen)
- ☐ **Antihistamine** (such as Benadryl®)
- ☐ **Anti-diarrheal** medicine: loperamide hydrochloride (Imodium®)
- ☐ **Blister treatment** (such as Moleskin or Compeed®)
- ☐ **Safety pins**
- ☐ **Baby powder** (helps with chafing)
- ☐ Small **scissors** and **tweezers**

PERSONAL ITEMS (OPTIONAL)

- ☐ **Travel wallet**: with passport/ID, health insurance card, pilgrim passport, money, credit cards, ATM card, etc. Stash an extra ATM card or wad of cash somewhere separate from your wallet.
- ☐ **Earplugs**: high quality noise-canceling earplugs are essential for a good night's sleep.
- ☐ **Mobile phone** and **charger** (see Phones and Internet p. 9)
- ☐ **Camera, charger, memory cards**, compact USB flash drive for backup
- ☐ **Journal with pen/pencil**: highly recommended for remembering the details of each day, reflecting more fully on the experience and recording contact info of new friends.
- ☐ **Tablet or e-reader:** useful for checking email and for pleasure reading without carrying heavy books. Photos of family and home are good conversation starters.
- ☐ **Book** for pleasure reading (just bring one and trade when you're done)
- ☐ **Plug/currency converter** for any electrical appliances (European plugs run on 220V with two round prongs. Most electronics run on 110-220V, labeled on device, requiring only a plug converter and not a currency converter.)
- ☐ **Zippered plastic bags or waterproof stuff sacks** for keeping electronics and other valuables dry and organized.
- ☐ **Pilgrim's shell**

Camino Primitivo

Blister Treatment
- Take a break, remove socks to let feet cool and dry out. Check for hot spots and address by applying moleskin, Compeed®, or duct tape to create an additional rubbing surface to protect the hot spot.
- If a blister forms, use a sterilized needle to puncture its edge near the skin and drain using sterile materials. Air dry and re-dress blister with sterile bandages.
- If the blister or surrounding area becomes infected over the course of several days (increasing red appearance, tenderness, pus, red streaks), seek medical attention.

For **dry and cracked feet**, consider wearing socks all the time to keep moisture in for cracks to heal. In severely painful cracks, a tiny bit of super glue can be helpful to hold the crack together, but make sure to clean the area thoroughly with soap, water, and antiseptic.

Impact-related injuries are common with the large amount of paved surfaces on the Camino. If your feet and joints are taking a pounding, consider reducing your daily distance, walking on the softer shoulder near the paved path, or adding walking poles and/or thicker socks.

The Trail: The paths that make up the Camino de Santiago covered in this book span over 400km (250 miles) and vary greatly in trail surface, grade, landscapes, ecosystem, and climate. Proportionately, the Camino has more paved surfaces than many hikers expect, contributing to stress on feet and joints. **P** Paved / **U** Unpaved designations in this book refer to most obvious walking surface. There may be unpaved shoulders or footpaths along paved roads.

Route Finding, Trail Markings, Maps and GPS → The Camino Primitivo is generally well marked, with a few sections where marks are more scarce and faded. The most common waymarks are painted yellow arrows →, though a variety of other markings exist in different regions that incorporate yellow arrows or scallops shells into posts or signs. The most difficult sections to navigate are through large cities, where routes are often poorly marked and Camino markers compete with other signs. For this reason, we've included a number of detailed city maps throughout this book, though note that the maps are representative and not

The path is well marked with yellow arrows.

PREPARING TO WALK THE CAMINO

exhaustive, without every street name. When there is more than one marked route option, we provide a brief overview of both options and show them numbered on the map. **GPS route files are on our website, as well as tips on smart phone navigation.**

Daily Stages and Regional Sections: This book organizes the Camino Primitivo into 13 daily stages averaging about 24km (15 miles) per day, with two additional daily stages connecting the Camino del Norte from Villaviciosa to Oviedo. The page spreads introducing each stage include a stage map, elevation profile, total distance, paved/unpaved (**P/U**) percentages, difficulty level (see below), time estimate (☺), and a list of towns with albergues/pilgrim lodging.

Stages begin and end at the main or largest albergue in the beginning and ending locality whenever possible. For mid-stage towns and points of interest without albergues, measurements are taken from the town center or main church, whichever is prominent or closest to the marked route. Cumulative stage distances are noted on the stage maps and correspond to distances listed in town listings and elevation charts. Distances for off-route accommodations or points of interest are indicated with a plus symbol (example: +1.3km). Towns list resources available, all the albergues, and a selection of private accommodations in varying price ranges.

Distances are measured in kilometers and meters. Estimated **walking time** for each stage assumes a pace of 3-4 km/hr (1.8-2.5 mph) with difficulty in terrain and elevation change considered. Factor extra time for breaks and exploration. Each day's stage route is assigned a **difficulty level** from 1-3. These ratings consider an "average" walker, who is reasonably fit but not necessarily athletic.

Length:
1m = 1yd or 3ft
100m ≈ 100yd
1km = 0.62 miles
10km = 6.2 miles
1.6km = 1 mile

▮☐☐ **Easy:** Slight elevation change, sturdy footing, water easily accessible
▮▮☐ **Moderate:** Some elevation change, moderately challenging terrain
▮▮▮ **Challenging:** Significant elevation change, possibly rocky or narrow path with less stable footing, water and other amenities may be scarce

This **map guidebook** is designed to be lightweight and minimalist. It provides detailed stage and city maps, pilgrim lodging as well as select hotels, listing of amenities in relevant towns and cities, and basic preparation, background information, and tips 💡 when helpful. This book does not include comprehensive route descriptions, extensive historical background information, nor all hotel listings.

Visit **caminoguidebook.com** for expanded planning information.

A1

VILLAVICIOSA TO POLA DE SIERO

26.9km (16.8mi), ⏱ **7.5-10 Hours**, **Difficulty:** ▬◼◻
P 68%, 18.4km, **U** 32%, 8.5km

A gravel road leading to Figares

💡 Leaving Villaviciosa on the Camino del Norte, this connecting route (A1 and A2) leads away from the coast inland to Oviedo. Enjoy views from the narrow dirt path above the "Valley of God" (Valdediós), or consider detouring through the valley to visit the Monastery of Santa María. Upon reaching La Campa at the top of the day's biggest climb, meander through a string of charming villages. After El Castru, dirt lanes and forested paths lead past La Ermita de Bienvenida and Puente Medieval de Recuna on the way to Pola de Siero.

⚠ **Route Option:** The Camino del Norte splits at Casquita. Straight ahead leads to Gijón along the coastal Norte route. Left leads inland to Oviedo—the traditional starting point of the Camino Primitivo. From Oviedo, you can continue on the Camino Primitivo to Santiago or return to the coast, rejoining the Camino del Norte in Avilés.

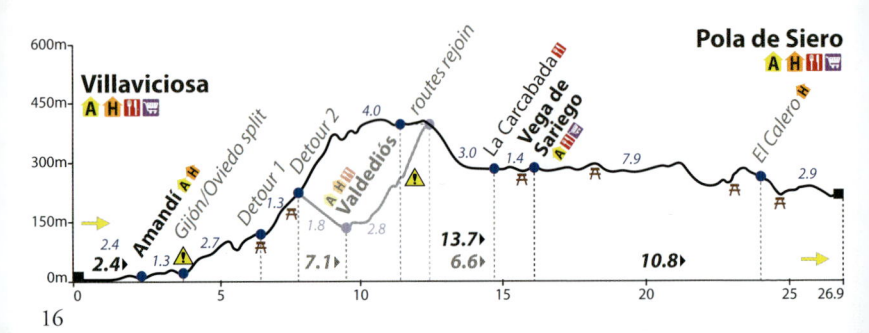

Camino del Norte Stage 21

Villaviciosa — A H ▯ 0.0

Amandí — A H 2.4

Routes split in Casquita (by "Sidra El Traviesu"): R to Gijón, L to Oviedo

Casquita 3.7

S. Juan Evangelista — AS-113

detour options to Valdediós

6.4

7.1

9.5

9.8 Arbazal

11.7 La Campa (12.3)

Figares

Valdediós — A H ▯

La Carcabada

Vega de Sariego — A H ▯

14.7 Pedrosa

16.1 Santianes

Aramanti

19.4 El Castru

AS-331

Aveno

El Cuito +450m — H

24.0

26.9 **Pola de Siero** — A H ▯

Amandí (inset)

AS-255

Casona 2

Ferrería 1

AS-267

Valdedios

100m

Pola de Siero (inset)

San Miguel 1

S. Antonio

Plaza Les Campes

Celleruelo

y Cajal

Asturias

Ramón

N-634

Loriga 2

V. León

M. de Canillejas

Nora

200m

A1   Camino Primitivo

⚠ **Route Option:** Two options to Valdediós leave the official route shortly after Casquita: 1) (6.4km) Turn R after a picnic area and follow the larger paved road up the valley to the monastery. 2) Continue on the official route uphill before turning R (7.4km) downhill to Valdediós. The second option requires more climbing but utilizes smaller roads.

The detours through Valdediós pass the Monastery of Santa María, replete with the 9th-century Iglesia de San Salvador (one of the better examples of pre-Romanesque architecture in Asturias), the 12th-century Iglesia de Santa María La Real, and the monastery cloister. A visit to all three costs €4 (⏲Tues-Sun; Apr 1- Sept 30 11am-1:30pm, 4:30-7pm; Oct 1-Mar 31 11am-1:30pm).

The official route skips the monastery and its churches but offers more pleasant walking on unpaved surfaces while affording wonderful views of the valley below. In wet weather, however, the dirt path can be quite muddy.

The climb to La Campa is long (on both the official route and the Valdediós alternate), but the route flattens considerably after La Campa. Be aware that the first reliably open café for a break after Villaviciosa is in La Carcabada (14.7km). Just ahead, Vega de Sariego makes a nice lunch spot.

After El Castru, don't miss the turn off the paved road onto dirt farm roads. Be careful on the short section on busy road AS-331 before continuing on forested paths. Shortly before Pola de Siero, pass the Ermita de La Bienvenida, whose name, according to tradition, comes from the historical practice of offering food (the "bienvenida" or welcome) to passing pilgrims. Now a picnic table at the church offers a welcoming break spot.

Not far ahead, a medieval bridge crosses the Recuna River. The bridge provided access from Pola de Siero to the Marcenado Malatería (a lepers hospital), which also provided services to sick or injured pilgrims.

2.4 Amandí A H
1. **A Ferrería** (🛏12, don 🏠): 🔣🍴🌐D📶☎, Ferrería 1, ☎646516846 📱, ⏲Mar-Oct, communal meals
2. **H Casona de Amandí** (€77-100/99-125): 🌐📶, San Juan Amandí 6, ☎985893411 📱

9.5 Valdediós A H🍴, on alternate route
To avoid the hustle and bustle of town, this is an excellent alternate end point in a very peaceful location.
1. ⭐**A Monasterio de Santa María de Valdediós** (par, 🛏22, €6): 🔣🍴☎, ☎681676335 📱, ⏲5-10pm all year, ring doorbell/call to enter earlier, dinner and breakfast from monastery for €10
2. **H Posada Samaritana de Valdediós** (€45/60 🏠): 🍴☎, ☎681676335 📱, Albergue and Posada run by same monastery, meals (lunch, dinner, breakfast) included in Posada pricing

16.1 Vega de Sariego 🅰🏨🛒➕📧🚌

If the walk from Villaviciosa to Pola de Siero seems long—especially considering the climb to La Campa—Vega de Sariego provides a nice alternate end point in a pleasant small town. From here, it's a flat 27.5km to Oviedo.

🅰 **Municipal** (🛏16, €5): 🏧📧, Plaza La Vega,
📞985748290 (bar), 📞985748003 (muni), 🕐all year, keys at Taberna La Casuca

24.0 El Cuito 🏨, +500m

🏨 **Casa Rural el Calero** (€35/55): 🅆🅳📶📧, Vega de Poja 37, 📞696287273, +500m

26.9 Pola de Siero 🅰🏨🍴🛒➕📧ℹ️🚌🚉, 🏷 Asturian: La Pola Siero

Pola de Siero was founded in 1270 by King Alfonso X. Prior to 1270, there was a pilgrim hostel that provided food and lodging. The town's founding charter granted a license to hold a weekly market, which proved important in the town's development. The market continues today, every Tuesday in Plaza Les Campes.

1. 🅰 **Casona de San Miguel** (muni, 🛏30, €6): 🏧📶📧, Celleruelo 57,
   📞609587772 (Antonio), 📞662596195 (Roberto), 📞628041915 (Manuel),
   🕐1:30-10pm all year, nice and clean with individual lockers
2. 🏨 **Loriga** (€35-50, 45-60): 🍴📶📧, Valeriano León 22, 📞985720026

Iglesia de San Salvador in Valdediós

POLA DE SIERO TO OVIEDO

16.7km (10.4mi), ⏱ **4-5.5 Hours**, **Difficulty:** ▬☐☐
🅿 93%, 15.6km, 🆄 7%, 1.1km

💡 Today's route passes through increasingly built-up towns and commercial area approaching Oviedo. Thankfully, the day is short and goes by quickly. Arrive in Oviedo early and enjoy the various sites that this capital city of Asturias has to offer!

3.3 Noreña 🏨🍴🛒➕🅔🚌🚉, +1.2km
🏨 **Cabeza** (€35-55/46-65): 🍴📶⊙, Javier Lauzurica 4, ☎985740274

Just before Meres (7.1km) a detour to the L passes an open-air chapel (Santuario Virgen de La Cabeza) with picnic tables outside, a nice break spot in good weather.

7.9 Meres 🏨🚉, +900m
🏨 **Zalle Don Fernando** (€50/60): 🍴📶⊙, Crta Oviedo-Santander km 8, ☎985986986 📧, +900m

10.9 Llugarín 🏨🍴🚌🚉✈, services off route
🏨 **Apartamentos Rurales Antojanes** (€60-94): 🅺🅆📶, Llugarín 10a, ☎985791280/670877763 📧, good reveiws, +200m

12.3 Colloto 🏨🍴🛒➕🅔🚌🚉
⚠ Exercise caution on the shoulder of N-634 before and after Colloto due to heavy traffic. Just before entering Colloto, cross over Puente Colloto, a 4th or 5th-century stone bridge. Shortly after passing Motel Abedules on the west edge of Colloto, take care not to miss the turn leaving N-634 onto a smaller paved road and then onto a paved walking path. This path skirts a busy and dangerous intersection before returning to N-634.
🏨 **Palacio de la Viñona** (€55+): 🍴🅆🅓📶⊙, Julian Clavería 14, ☎985793399 📧, +175m
🏨 **Abedules** (40+/43+): 🍴📶⊙, Caretera Colloto-Santander 70, ☎985793998 📧, on N-634 as you leave Colloto

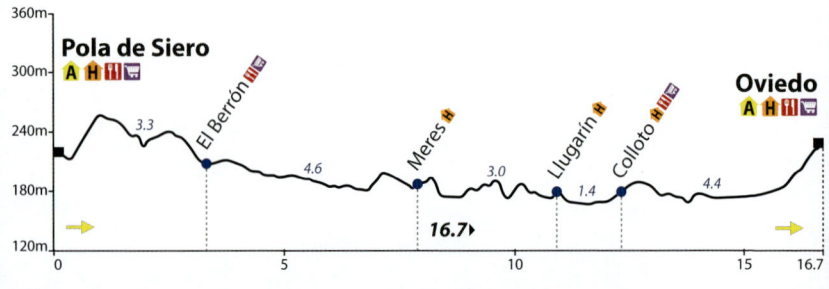

Pola de Siero

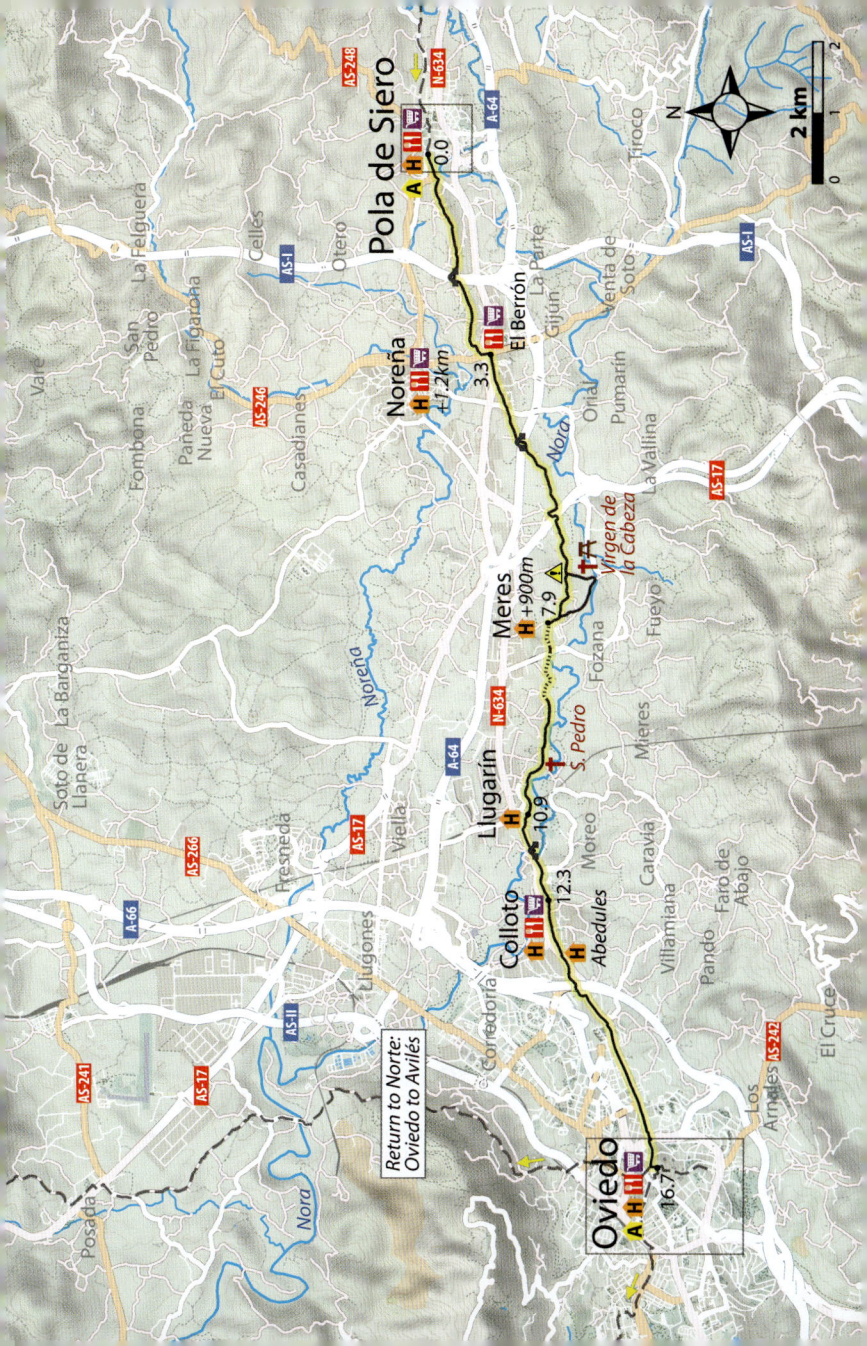

Noreña ±1.2 km

El Berrón — 3.3

Meres +900 m — 7.9

Virgen de la Cabeza

S. Pedro

Llugarín — 10.9

Colloto — 12.3

Abedules

Return to Norte: Oviedo to Avilés

Oviedo — 16.7

16.7 Oviedo

Waymarks are sparse approaching Oviedo, but navigation is simple. Stay on N-634 (c/Tenderina Alta) uphill entering the city. Pass Hotel Astures on the L and continue on c/Azcárraga and then c/Jovellanos to reach Monasterio de San Pelayo and Catedral de San Salvador on the L. The municipal albergue is 900m from the cathedral.

The Kingdom of Asturias began in 720, with King Pelayo's revolt against Muslim rule in Spain. Oviedo (Uviéu in Asturian) was founded by the monks Máximo and Froimestano under the reign of Fruela I in 761. Alfonso II "The Chaste" (791-842) later recognized Oviedo as the capital of the Kingdom of Asturias (and by extension Christian Spain) and created the first major pilgrimage route to Santiago, which started from Oviedo, hence the route's name today: The Camino Primitivo or "The Original Way".

Oviedo still serves as the capital of Asturias and is the administrative and commercial center of the region. The city has rich architectural history, with several beautiful churches within and just outside the city. The Cathedral of San Salvador stands in the center of Oviedo. Founded in 782 and enlarged in 802, the main structure that you see today was built primarily between the 14th and 16th centuries. Within the cathedral, the Cámara Santa (or Holy Chamber) dates back to the 9th century and contains several important relics.

In addition to many other churches, there are three 9th century, pre-Romanesque churches in or outside Oviedo designated as UNESCO World Heritage sites. The oldest and largest, San Julián de los Prados, lies closest to the city center and is renowned for its frescoes. Santa María del Naranco and San Miguel de Lillo are located 3km outside the city center on a hillside. In addition to their exquisite architecture, the churches offer views of the surrounding area.

1. **El Salvador** (muni, 51, €6): Leopoldo Alas 20, 985228525, 4-10pm, +900m, credenciales and water-resistant cases for sale, disposable sheets cost extra
2. **La Peregrina** (42, €10): Gascona 18, 687133932, all year, moved to new location in 2018
3. **Ovetense** (€35/45): San Juan 6, 985220840
4. **Pensión Fidalgo** (€35-50): Jovellanos 5, 985213287
5. **Campoamor** (€65-130): Argüelles, 23, 985210720
6. **NH Oviedo Principado** (€65-130): San Francisco 6, 985217792
7. **City Express Covadonga** (€35/45): Calle Covadonga 7, 985203232
8. **Hostal San Juan** (€20-26/30-35): Calle Palacio Valdés 4, 985215422
9. **Pensión Romero** (€25/40): Uria 36, 985227591
10. **Santa Cruz** (€35/48): Santa Cruz 6, 985223711
11. **Hostal Rosal** (€35-40/45-50): Cabo Noval 2, 985205328
12. **Nap Hotel Carta Puebla** (€35/46): Carta-Puebla 6, 985080800
13. **Hostal Álvarez** (€27-37/35-50): Independencia 14, 985252673
14. **Favila** (€30-40/40-50): Uria 37, 985253877
15. **Pensión Oviedo** (€25-35/35-45): Uria 43, 985241000
16. **Confort** (€35/50): Joaquina Bobela 3, 985118556

Oviedo

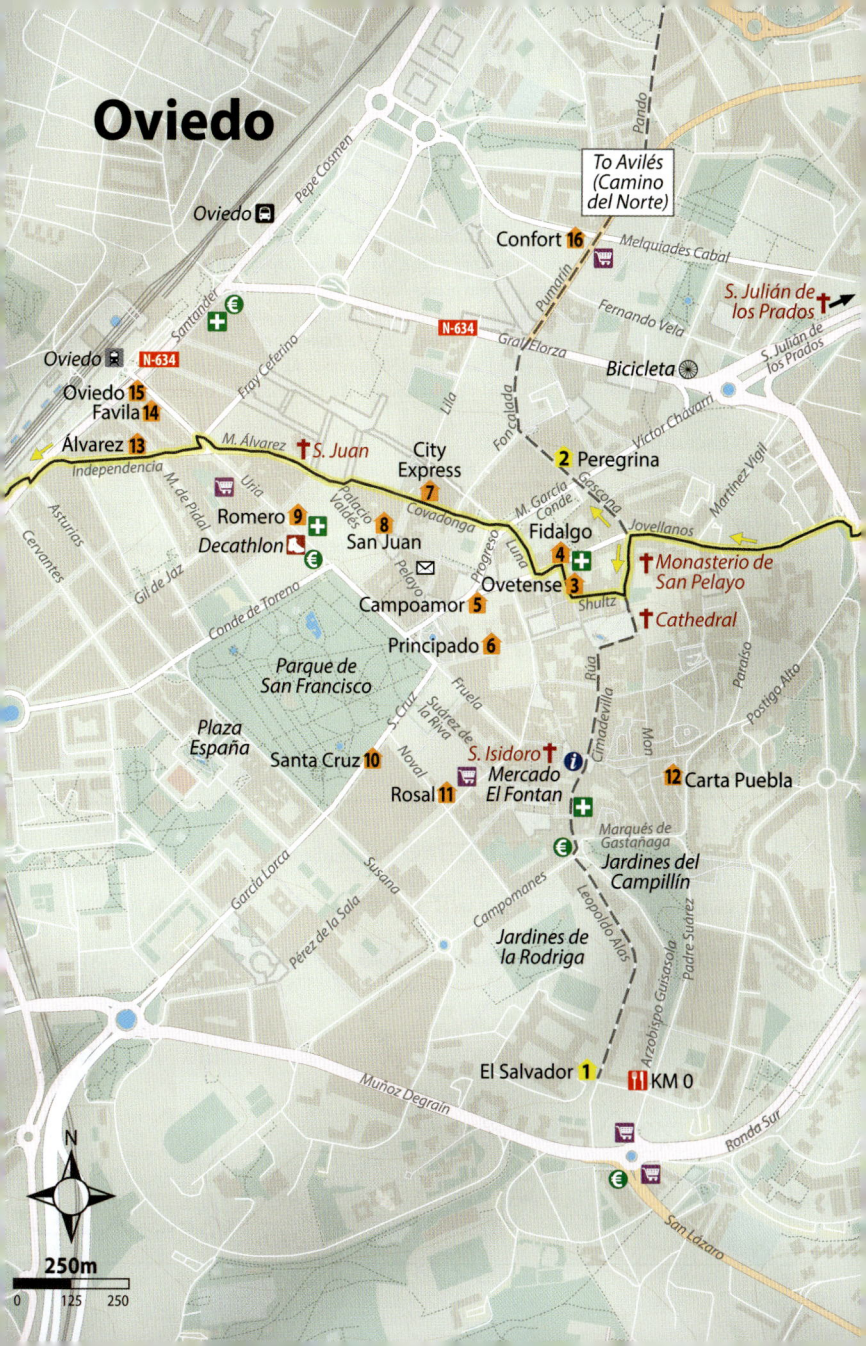

- Oviedo 🚌
- To Avilés (Camino del Norte)
- Confort **16**
- Melquiades Cabal
- Pepe Cosmen
- Santander
- Fray Ceferino
- Pumarín
- Fernando Vela
- S. Julián de los Prados ✝
- N-634
- Gral. Elorza
- Bicicleta
- S. Julián de los Prados
- Oviedo 🚆 N-634
- Oviedo **15**
- Favila **14**
- Álvarez **13**
- M. Álvarez ✝ S. Juan
- City Express
- **2** Peregrina
- Víctor Chávarri
- Martínez Vigil
- Independencia
- Uría
- **7**
- Covadonga
- M. García Conde
- Gascona
- Jovellanos
- Romero **9**
- Palacio Valdés
- **8**
- Fidalgo
- Monasterio de San Pelayo ✝
- Decathlon
- San Juan
- Progreso
- Luna
- **4**
- Pelayo
- Ovetense **3**
- Shultz
- ✝ Cathedral
- M. de Pidal
- Campoamor **5**
- Asturias
- Conde de Toreno
- Principado **6**
- Gil de Jaz
- Parque de San Francisco
- Fuela
- Cervantes
- Plaza España
- S. Cruz
- Suárez de la Riva
- Cimadevilla
- Mon
- Postigo Alto
- Paraíso
- Santa Cruz **10**
- Noval
- S. Isidoro ✝ ℹ
- Mercado El Fontán
- **12** Carta Puebla
- Rosal **11**
- Marqués de Gastañaga
- Jardines del Campillín
- García Lorca
- Susana
- Campomanes
- Pérez de la Sala
- Jardines de la Rodriga
- Leopoldo Alas
- Padre Suárez
- Arzobispo Guisasola
- El Salvador **1**
- 🍴 KM 0
- Muñoz Degrain
- Ronda Sur
- San Lázaro

N

250m
0 125 250

1 OVIEDO TO GRADO

25.5km (15.9mi), ⏱ 7-9 Hours, Difficulty: ▮▮▯
🅿 75%, 19.1km, 🆄 25%, 6.4km

💡 Leave Oviedo's city sprawl behind to follow smaller roads and dirt tracks. Enjoy views of the Cordillera Cantábrica mountain range to the south, a constant companion in the distance for much of the way. There are few waymarks (other than occasional bronze shells) leaving Oviedo (city map p. 23). From the cathedral, go north and turn L immediately onto c/Shultz. Take the first R onto c/San Juan. Turn L onto c/Jovellanos, then a quick R onto c/Luna. Continue onto c/Santa Clara, c/Covadonga, c/Melquiades Álvarez (passing Iglesia de San Juan), and c/Independencia. Waymarks begin again at Av. de Santander by the train stations.

12.2 Escamplero A H 🍴🛒
Possible alternate end point with restaurant, basic shop and lodging options.
1. **A Municipal** (🛏30, €5): 🚿⊙, ☎985799005 (El Tendejón), 🗓all year, keys at Pensión/Restaurante El Tendejón or at local store on Wednesdays
2. **H El Tendejón** (€35): 🍴📶⊙, ☎985799005, 🗓reservations required on Wednesdays

17.9 Vega de Ano H🍴🛒🚌🚉, +1.1km
For the bar in Valduno, follow a dirt path leaving the main route to L at the bottom of a descent on a dirt path following a stream (17.9km). Just past the bar to the R are remains of Roman baths behind Capilla de Santa Eulalia. To reach Vega de Ano, cross the Río Nalón.
H Casa Celesto (€15/30): 🍴📶⊙, N-634, ☎985751893

23.5 Sestiello H🍴, +1.3km
H El Lacayo (€30-58/40-68): 🍴📶, Sestiello 1, ☎985753566 📧

25.5 Grado A H 🍴🛒🏧➕©🚌🚉
1. **A ⭐Municipal** (🛏16, don 💶): 🚿🅆🄳📶⊙, Maestra Benicia 1, ☎985752766 📧, 🗓mid Mar-Oct, nice kitchen, very hospitable
2. **A La Quintada** (🛏24 beds, €12): 🚿🅆🄳📶⊙, Eulogio Díaz de Miranda 30, ☎640377256 📧, 🗓12pm Mar-Nov
3. **H Cá Teo** (€10/20): 🚿📶⊙, Vistalegre 22, ☎685-182412/649603155, 🗓May-Oct
4. **H Auto Bar** (€20/30): 🍴📶⊙, Flórez Estrada 29, ☎985752678 📧, 🗓all year

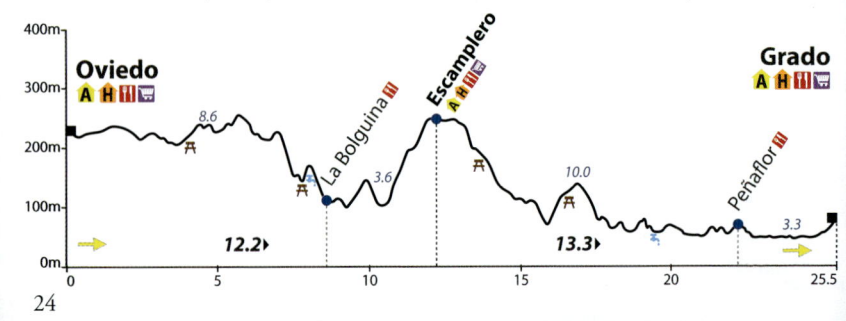

Map: Oviedo to Grado

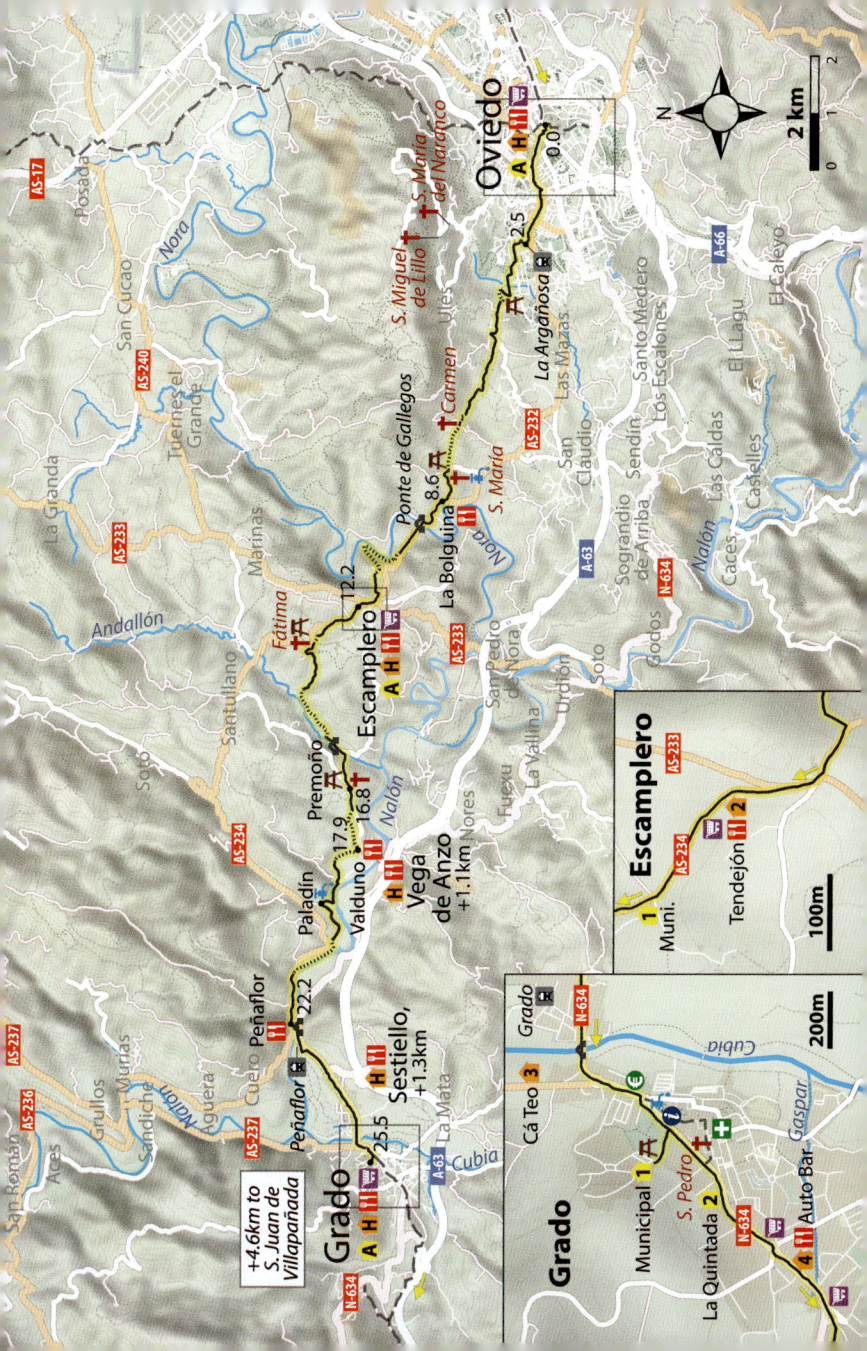

N · 2 km scale

Main route (Oviedo → Grado)

- **Oviedo** — A H ¶ — 0.0
- 2.5
- S. María del Naranco †
- S. Miguel de Lillo †
- La Argañosa
- Ules
- Carmen †
- Ponte de Gallegos — 8.6
- S. María †
- La Bolguina
- AS-233
- Fátima †
- 12.2
- **Escamplero** — A H ¶
- Premoño †
- 16.8 ¶
- 17.9
- Valduno H ¶
- Paladín
- **Vega de Anzo** ¶ +1.1km Nores
- Cueto Peñaflor ¶
- 22.2
- **Peñaflor** ¶
- AS-237
- Sestiello, +1.3km H ¶
- 25.5
- La Mata
- Cubia
- **Grado** A H ¶
- +4.6km to S. Juan de Villapañada
- N-634

Rivers/places: Posada, Nora, San Cucao, Tuernes el Grande, La Granda, AS-240, AS-17, AS-233, Marinas, Andallón, Santullano, Soto, AS-234, Murias, AS-236, Grullos, AS-237, Ambás, Sandiche, Aguera, Nalón, San Pedro de Nora, La Vallina, Fresnu, Urdón, Godos, Caces, N-634, Sograndio de Arriba, Santo Medero, Los Escalones, Sendin, San Claudio, Las Mazas, A-66, El Lagu, El Caleyo, Castielles, Las Caldas, Nalón, A-63

Inset: Escamplero

- AS-233
- Tendejón ¶
- AS-234
- Muni. 1
- 100m

Inset: Grado

- N-634
- Cá Teo 3
- Grado
- Cubia
- Gaspar
- Municipal 1 †
- S. Pedro †
- La Quintada 2
- N-634
- Auto Bar 4 ¶
- 200m

GRADO TO SALAS

2

22.7km (14.2mi), ⏱ **6.5-8.5 Hours, Difficulty:** ▬▢▢
P 58%, 13.2km, U 42%, 9.5km

An abandoned stone hut beside a dirt track leading to Doriga

💡 Be prepared for the 350m climb out of Grado. Take it easy and enjoy the wonderful views! Much like yesterday, the way follows rural paved roads and dirt tracks through rolling Asturian countryside. You still haven't truly reached the mountains!

3.7 San Juan A, +900m
A ⭐ **Municipal** (🛏20, €5): 🇰🇼🅾, 📞670596854, ⏱2-10pm all year, incredible views, peaceful location, vending machine with coffee/snacks

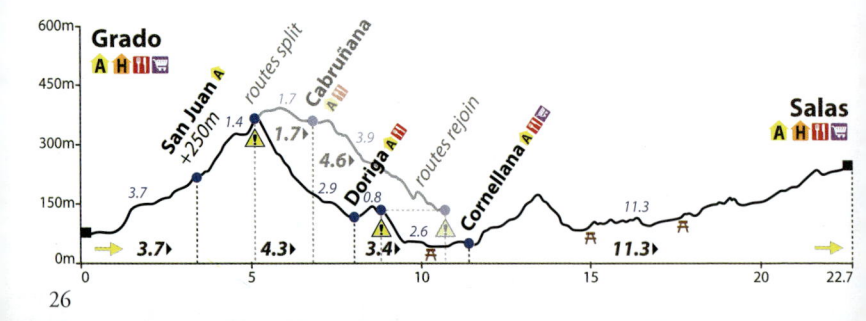

26

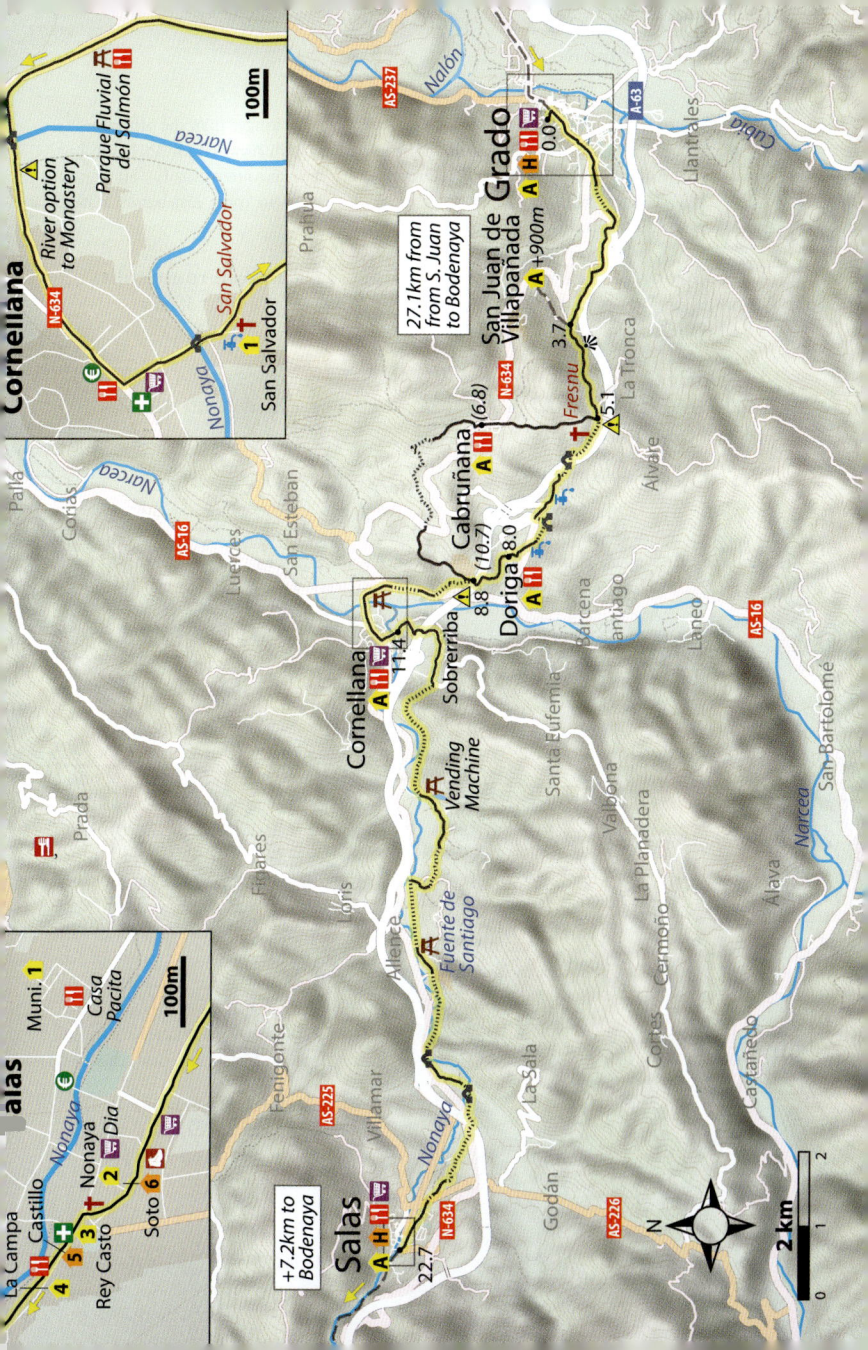

Cornellana

- Parque Fluvial del Salmón
- River option to Monastery
- San Salvador
- Narcea
- Nonaya
- N-634
- AS-16
- AS-237

100m

Salas

- La Campa
- Castillo
- Rey Casto
- Nonaya
- Soto
- Muni: 1
- Casa Pacita
- Dia
- Fenigonte
- Villamar
- AS-225

100m

+7.2km to Bodenaya

Salas
A · H · ¶
22.7
N-634

Nonaya
La Sala
Godán
AS-226

Fuente de Santiago
Vending Machine
Allence

Cornellana
A · H · ¶
11.4

Sobrerriba
8.8

Doriga
A · ¶
8.0

Cabruñana
A · ¶
(10.7)
(6.8)

Fresnu
N-634
5.1
La Tronca
3.7

San Juan de Villapañada
A +900m

27.1km from from S. Juan to Bodenaya

Grado
A · H · ¶
0.0
A-63
Llantrales
Cubia
Nalón

Narcea
Palla
Cotias
Luerces
San Esteban
Prada
Piñares
Oris
Santa Eufemia
Barcena
Santiago
Laneo
La Planadera
Valbona
Cormeño
Corpes
Álava
Castañedo
San-Bartolomé
Alvare
AS-16

N
2km
0 1 2

Camino Primitivo

⚠️ **Route Option:** An alternate route via Cabruñana is 1.9km longer than the official route and spends more time on paved roads. At the top of the climb from Grado (5.1km), just below the Santuario de Nuestra Señora de Fresnu, the alternate route turns R, following a paved road 1.7km to Cabruñana. The alternate rejoins the main route just before a steep descent along a dirt path to AS-16.

6.8 Cabruñana 🅰️🍴, on alternate route (+1.7km from route split)
🅰️ **Municipal** (🛏18, €5): 🇰 🇼 🇴, Alto de Cabruñana, ☎985750037, 🕐all year, adjacent to restaurant with pilgrim menu

8.0 Doriga 🅰️🍴
🅰️ **CáPacita** (🛏10, €12): 🇼 🇴, ☎684613861, 🕐all year, rooms above cafe/restaurant, call in shoulder seasons, mixed reviews

11.4 Cornellana 🅰️🍴🛒➕🏧📧

Cornellana makes a nice spot for a lunch break. There's a nice picnic area at the Parque Fluvial del Salmón before crossing the Narcea River and entering Cornellana. The benches outside Monasterio de San Salvador also make a great lunch spot. (There's a water spigot just to the R of the monastery as you face it with the river at your back.)

At the entrance to town, a paved walking path (P.R. AS-128) leads directly to the monastery along the Narcea River, but this skips all the town's services.

Monasterio de San Salvador was founded by Infanta Cristina (daughter of King Bermudo II and Queen Velasquita) in 1024 and was donated to the Abbey of Cluny in 1122. The Romanesque church was renovated in the 17th century, and more recent renovation efforts have sought to preserve the structures. The image of a bear feeding a child on the garden door alludes to a popular legend about Cristina that she survived under the protection of a bear after being lost in the Asturian forest. Exterior visits only.

🅰️ **Monasterio de San Salvador** (muni, 🛏30, €5): 🇰 🇼 🇩 📶 🇴, ☎635485932, 🕐2-10pm all year, good value and pleasant location

Santa María la Mayor Collegiate in Salas

22.7 Salas

Salas is a beautiful medieval town, which dates back to 1120 when Queen Urraca granted a castle here. Salas was (and is!) a major stopping point along the Camino Primitivo. Records of a pilgrim hostel date back to 1405.

Salas boasts beautiful architecture in its city center. The 16th-century Santa María la Mayor Collegiate is a wonderful example of Renaissance architecture in the area and contains a mausoleum to Fernando Valdés Salas (founder of Oviedo University and Inquisitor General), made in the late 16th century by Italian sculptor Pompeyo Leoni. Across the plaza a low stone archway connects the Valdés Salas palace (16th century; Valdés Salas family home, now containing a hotel and cultural center) and tower (15th century).

1. **Municipal** (16, €5): La Veiga 8, 675767969 (for stamps), all year, keys in Casa Pacita, quite simple, mixed reviews
2. **Valle de Nonaya** (20, €10): Arzobispo Valdés Salas 5, 626527073, 12pm all year
3. **Rey Casto** (20, €10): Plaza del Ayuntamiento 18, 985830261/670440909, 12-8pm (reception) Apr-Oct, very pleasant/hospitable, nice views of church
4. **La Campa** (30, €10/35): Plaza de la Campa 7, 984885019, 12-10:30pm Mar 15-Oct 15, ownership change in 2018—name may change but location same, vegetarian and healthy food options
5. **Castillo de Valdés Salas** (€50/70): Plaza de La Campa, 985830173, all year except for Oct 15-30, discounts for pilgrims
6. **Soto** (€20/35): Arzobispo Valdés 9, 985830037, all year

💡 Bodenaya and its wonderful albergue make a nice alternate end point if you still have strength left in your legs (7.2km past Salas, with a long climb).

3

SALAS TO TINEO

19.8km (12.4mi), ⏲ **6-8 Hours**, **Difficulty:** ▬▬☐
🅿 36%, 7.2km, Ⓤ 64%, 12.6km

Leaving Salas on a dirt track above the Nonaya River

💡 Today you begin to enter the mountains in earnest. Leave Salas along a dirt road following the Nonaya River. The *Cascada Nonaya* (Nonaya Waterfall) is well worth a brief detour. Climb to Bodenaya, which boasts a wonderful albergue. Continue through La Espina, a traditional pilgrim stopping point, and follow dirt roads along a hillside to Tineo, a town perched in a beautiful location above a mountain valley.

7.2 Bodenaya Ⓐ

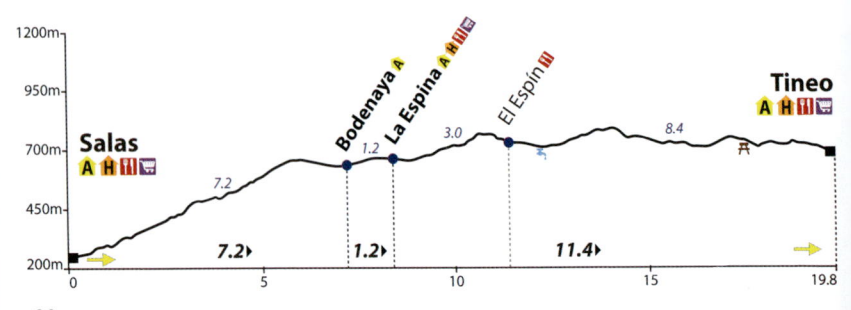

If you sleep in Bodenaya, Bodenaya to Campiello (25.3km) makes a good following stage.
Ⓐ ⭐ **Bodenaya** (⇱18, don 💶): 🅺🍴🛏︎Ⓦ🅳📶⊙, 📞645888984, 🕓Feb/Mar-Nov, communal dinner and breakfast

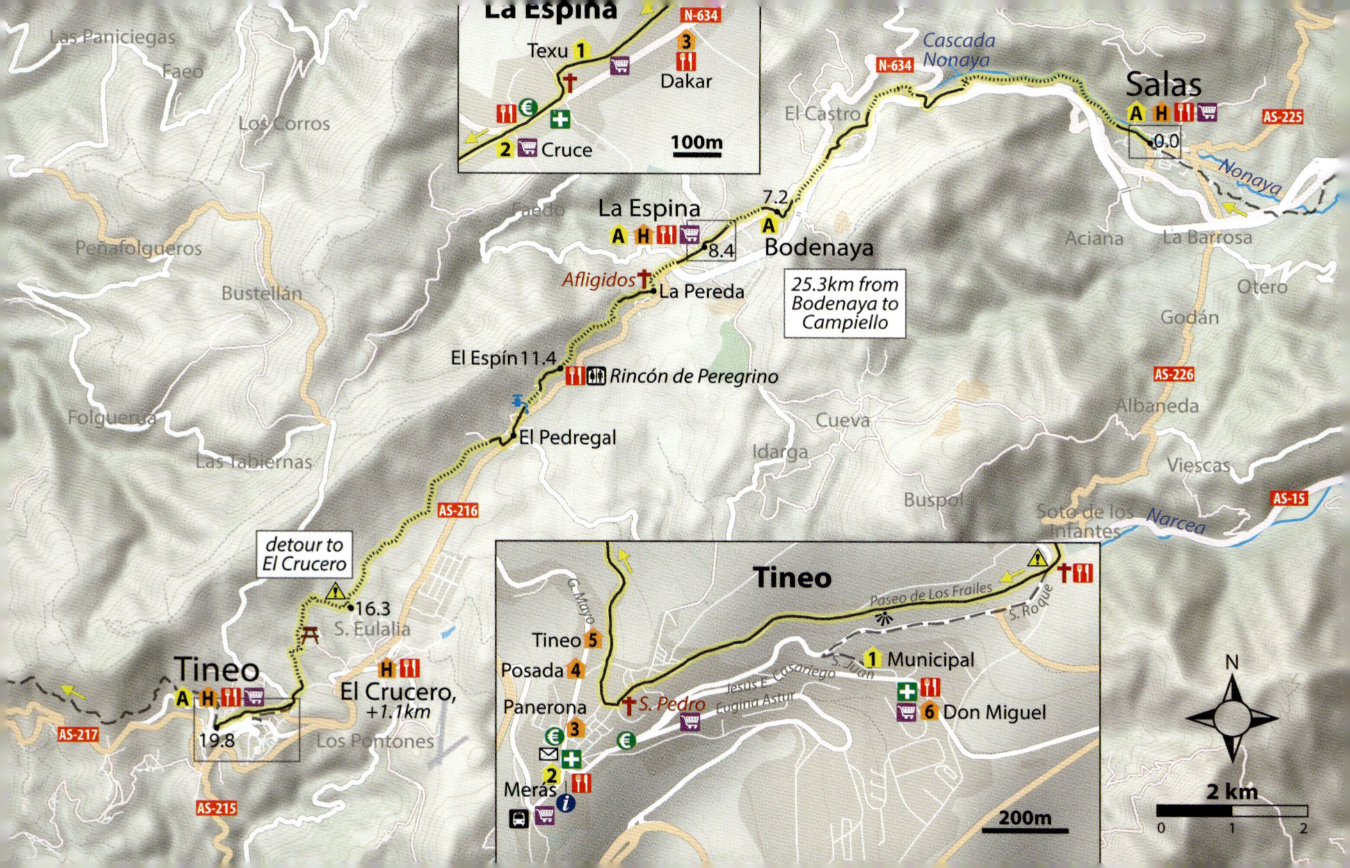
La Espina
Texu 1
3
Dakar
2 Cruce
100m
N-634
Salas
0.0
AS-225
Nonaya
Cascada Nonaya
El Castro
La Espina
7.2
8.4
Bodenaya
Afligidos
La Pereda
25.3km from Bodenaya to Campiello
El Espín 11.4
Rincón de Peregrino
El Pedregal
AS-216
detour to El Crucero
16.3
S. Eulalia
Tineo
19.8
El Crucero, +1.1km
Los Pontones
AS-217
AS-215
Las Paniciegas
Faeo
Los Corros
Peñafolgueros
Bustellán
Folgueira
Las Tabiernas
Faedo
Aciana
La Barrosa
Otero
Godán
AS-226
Albaneda
Cueva
Idarga
Viescas
Buspol
Soto de los Infantes
Narcea
AS-15
Tineo
Paseo de Los Frailes
S. Roque
G. Mayo
Tineo 5
Posada 4
Panerona 3
1 Municipal
S. Juan
Jesús E. Casariego
Eugina Astur
S. Pedro
6 Don Miguel
2
Merás
200m
N
2 km
0
1
2

8.4 La Espina

1. **El Texu** (🛏12, €10/18/24): Plaza de la Iglesia 6, ☎603751906, meals available for donation, washer/dryer €5 together
2. **El Cruce** (🛏14, don): ☎639365210/985837381, ⊙all year, above grocery store (the owner, Carmen, runs albergue), good reviews
3. **Pensión Dakar** (€15/24-30): Constitución 41, ☎985837062, €9 menú

In El Espín (11.4km), a small enclosed building with tables and vending machines (El Rincón de Peregrino) provides a dry break area on rainy days. A small bathroom is located just before the building.

16.3 El Crucero, +1.1km

Casa Lula (€25/40): El Crucero 10, ☎985801600,
Rindión (€30+/40+): El Crucero 49, ☎600532699

19.8 Tineo

At Bar la Casina and Ermita de San Roque (before Tineo), you can either continue straight on the official route (Paseo de Los Frailes) or follow a paved road L to reach the municipal albergue. Most of the waymarks direct you to the municipal albergue, but if you're not staying there, the official route offers a more pleasant walk into Tineo with excellent views out over the town.

Tineo dates back to Roman times and was a major pilgrim stop in the Middle Ages. A decree by Alfonso IX in 1222 made stops in Tineo and the Monastery of Obona (8.0km past Tineo) compulsory. In the center of town, the Iglesia de San Pedro—once the location of a Franciscan monastery (Convento de San Francisco de Monte)—houses the Museo de Arte Sacro and its collection of religious art from the region.

1. **Mater Christi** (muni, 🛏31, €5): Cabezas de San Juan, ☎628237312, ⊙2-10pm all year, stamps at 5:30pm, simple, bit crowded, mixed reviews
2. **Palacio de Merás** (🛏54, €12/40+/50+): Pío Cuervo 3, ☎985900111, ⊙12pm all year, sauna, pilgrim menu
4. **Apartamentos La Panerona** (€50): González Mayo 4, ☎985801228/635173760, complete apartments, minimum 2-night stay
5. **Pensión la Posada** (€25-30/35-40): González Mayo 25, ☎985800410, good reviews
6. **Pensión Bar Tineo** (€25/30): González Mayo 28, ☎985800710
7. **Don Miguel** (€20/30): Oviedo 6, ☎985800325

⚠ Stages 4-5 Route Options

Looking ahead at the coming two days, a major split offers two route options at the end of stage 4 (soon after Borres). The Caminos diverge for only 14-18km, but overnight in different towns, so we've organized the Tineo-Berducedo section into two different two-stage options (4-5 and 4a-5a).

❶ ★Via Hospitales: Stages 4-5 (2 days, 39.9km)

Stage 4: Tineo to Borres 15.6km, Stage 5: Borres to Berducedo 24.3km

The traditional high route climbs from the split and follows a ridgeline past the remains of a number of pilgrim *hospitales* (pilgrim hostels). This remote option affords stunning views in all directions—the best of the entire Camino Primitivo. There are no services along this route after Borres, so you'll have to carry all your food and water from Borres to Berducedo (24.3km). What's more, the 15.2km from Borres to Puerto del Palo (a pass where the two route options rejoin) are remote and generally far from road access.

We recommend the Hospitales route as long as you feel comfortable braving its challenges—the walk is magnificent! Still, both options offer some of the finest walking of the entire Camino Primitivo. You can't go wrong with either. ⚠ If you're walking via Hospitales, 🍴 Bar El Barín in Borres is the last certain place for food/water before Berducedo (24.3km). The bar can supply packed lunches.

❷ Via Pola de Allande: Stages 4A-5A (2 days, 44.4km)

Stage 4A: Tineo to Pola de Allande 26.6, Stage 5A: Pola de Allande to Berducedo 17.8km

After the routes split, the "official" path stays lower and, after passing through rolling countryside, descends to Pola de Allande before climbing back to Puerto del Palo. This option is actually 4.5km longer and has more total climbing than the route via Hospitales. The Pola de Allande option does offer more frequent access to services. It's also advisable to follow this route in foggy/inclement weather and may be the only option for winter or shoulder season walking due to the possibility of snow on the Hospitales route.

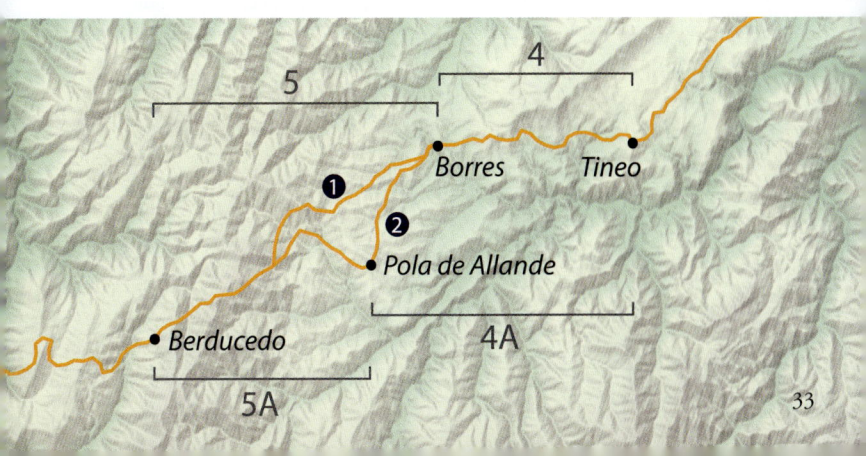

TINEO TO BORRES ❶

15.6km (9.8mi), ⏱ 4-5.5 Hours, Difficulty: ▬☐☐
🅿 41%, 6.4km, Ⓤ 59%, 9.2km

⚠ See p. 33 for route option descriptions for stages 4-5.

💡 Leave Tineo and after passing Fuente de San Juan (a nice spot for a break, complete with picnic tables) continue along dirt paths with stunning views over the valley below. After the initial climb from Tineo to the day's high point at just over 900m, continue (mostly on dirt roads and tracks) through rural countryside on the way to Borres. The Obona Monastery, a traditional pilgrim stopping point, is well worth a 350m detour (each way).

8.0 Monasterio de Obona, +350m
This monastery was a mandatory pilgrim stopping point by Alfonso IX's decree. A primitive worship building at the site dates back to 780, while the main church construction began in the 13th century. The 18th-century monastery (now in ruins) has records of a monastic community in the area as far back as the 11th century.

12.7 Campiello 🅰 🅷 🍴 🛒
If you plan to stay in Borres during the summer months, it's advisable to call ahead to Bar El Barín from Campiello to see if the municipal albergue in Borres (only 19 beds) has filled up. There are plenty of beds in Campiello, and staying here only adds 2.9km to the following day's walk. While the bar in Borres can make packed lunches, consider restocking on supplies in Campiella. Both albergues (each on route) have well-supplied grocery stores.

🅰 🅷 **Casa Hermina** (📞26, €8/30-40/40-50): 🍴🛒Ⓦ🅳📶Ⓞ, Campiello 15, 📞985800011, ⊙all year, 🍞 breakfast €3, 📶 wifi in bar

🅰 🅷 **Casa Ricardo** (📞26, €10/25/35): 🍴🛒Ⓦ🅳📶Ⓞ, Campiello 1, 📞985801776/622402358, ⊙all year (except for Sundays in Dec-Feb)

15.6 Borres 🅰 🍴
🅰 **Municipal** (📞19, €5): 🛒Ⓞ, 📞663785266, ⊙all year, 150m to R uphill from Fonte La Reguera, registration in Bar El Barín, simple but sufficient, fill water at bar

Stage 4A details and accommodations on p. 36.
Stage 5 continues on p. 38.

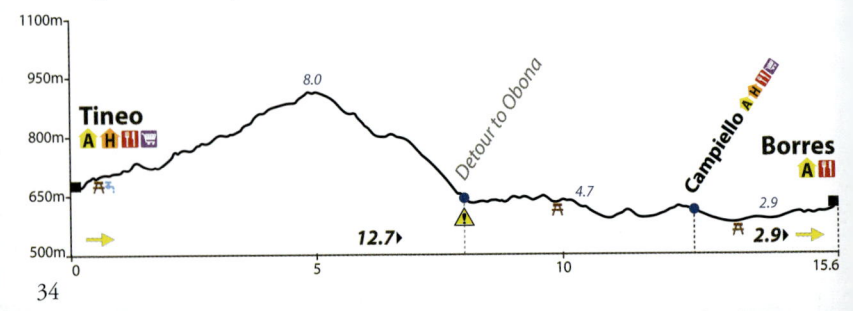

Tineo

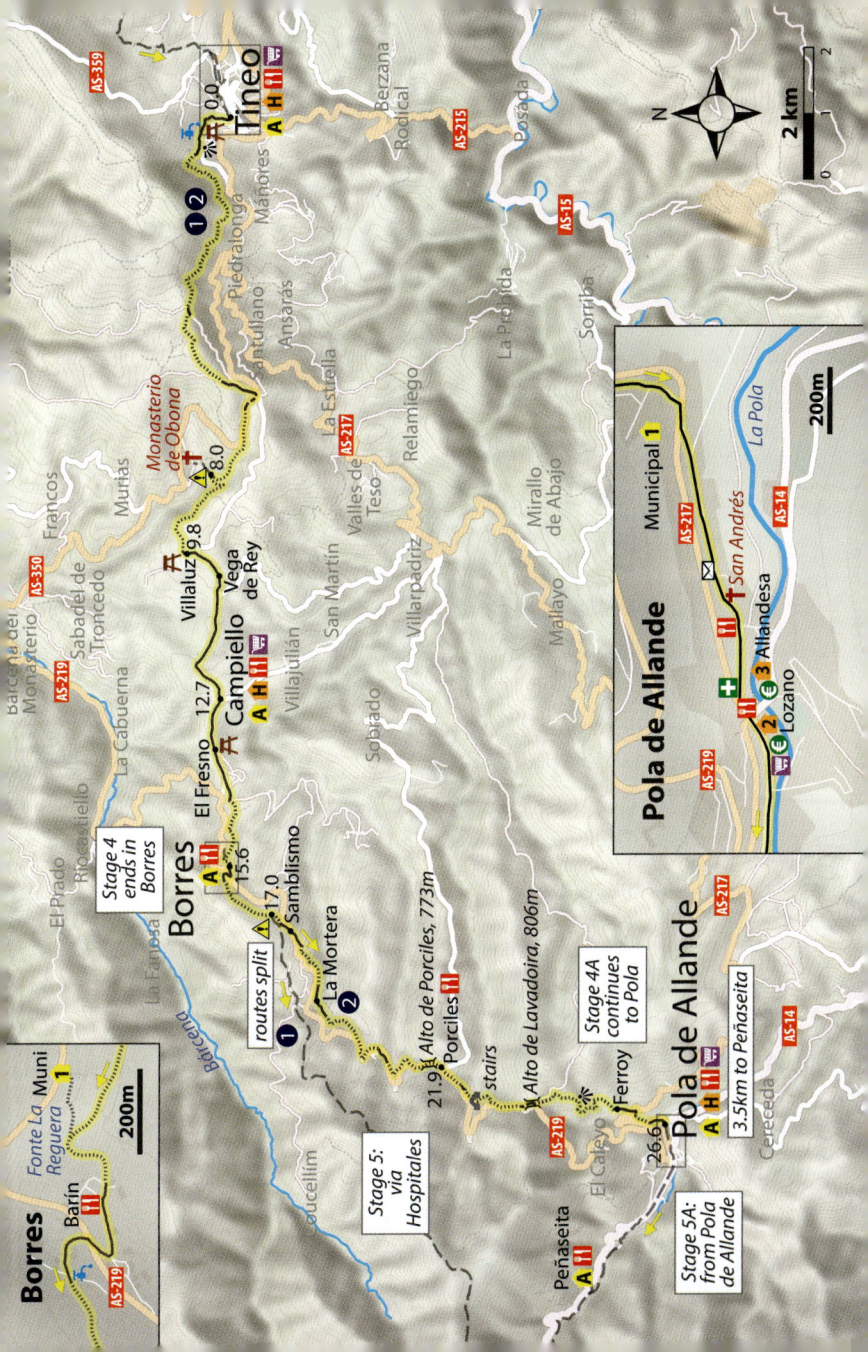

AS-359
AS-215
AS-15
AS-217
AS-350
AS-219

Piedralonga
Berzana
Rodical
Posada
Santullano
Ansarás
La Estrella
Relamiego
Valles de Teso
Mallayo
Mirallo de Abajo
La Pérdida
Soriba
Monasterio de Obona 8.0
Villaluz 9.8
Vega de Rey
Campiello 12.7
San Martín
Villajulián
Villarpadriz
Sobrado

El Fresno
Murías
Francos
Sabadell de Troncedo
La Cabuerna
Ricocastiello
El Prado
La Fanesa

Stage 4 ends in Borres

Borres 15.6
Samblismo 17.0
La Mortera
routes split

21.9 Alto de Porciles, 773m
Porciles
stairs
Alto de Lavadoira, 806m
Ferroy
26.6 **Pola de Allande**
El Cajeyo
Cereceda
Peñaseita
3.5km to Peñaseita

Stage 5: via Hospitales

Stage 4A continues to Pola

Stage 5A: from Pola de Allande

AS-217
AS-219
AS-14

Pola de Allande

Municipal 1
San Andrés
Allandesa
Lozano
La Pola
AS-217
AS-14
AS-219
200m

Borres

Fonte La Muni Reguera 1
Barín
AS-219
200m

N
2 km
0 — 2

4A TINEO TO POLA DE ALLANDE ❷

26.6km (16.6mi), 🕐 **8-10 Hours**, Difficulty: ▪️▪️🟧
🅿 34%, 9.1km, Ⓤ 66%, 17.5km

💡 Follow the information and details from stage 4 (p. 34-35) through Campiello and Borres. Continue onward for 1.4km past Borres to where the route splits for Pola de Allande.

12.7 Campiello A H 🍴🛒🏠, see p. 34-35

15.6 Borres A 🍴, see p. 34-35

26.6 Pola de Allande A H 🍴🛒➕€🏠, map p. 35
1. **A Municipal** (💤24, €6): 🚿◯, América 46, 📞663324783, 646832425 (Miguel Angel), 🕐all year, call # on door if locked, simple, but functional
2. **H La Nueva Allandesa** (€30/50 🚿): 🍴📶◯, Donato Fernandez 3, 📞985807027/985807312 📧, highly-regarded restaurant/menu
3. **H Lozano** (€25/40): 🍴📶◯, Galicia 5, 📞985807102/985807768 📧, pilgrim menu

Descending to Pola de Allande (left), Nisón River after Pola de Allande (right)

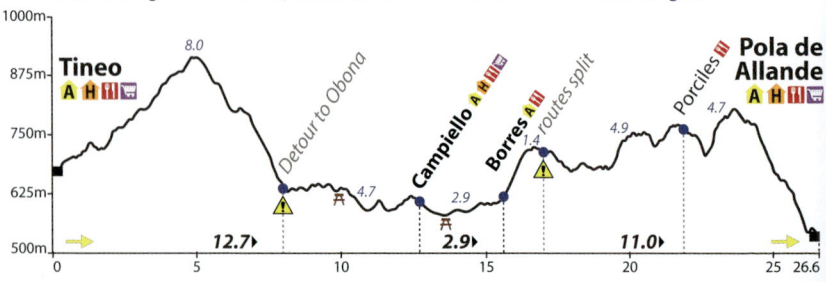

POLA DE ALLANDE TO BERDUCEDO ❷

5A

17.8km (11.1mi), ⏱ **6-7.5 Hours**, Difficulty: ▬◻◻
🅿 18%, 3.3km, 🆄 82%, 14.5km

💡 For 5A stage map, see p. 39. Follow a beautiful forested pathway to climb through the valley beside the Nisón River. Enjoy some expansive views and leave the forests behind to approach Puerto del Palo (1147m), where you rejoin the Hospitales route. Descend steeply on a dirt path and continue through the abandoned village of Montefurado. The Capilla de Montefurado at the entrance of the village was once a pilgrim hospital.

3.2 Peñaseita 🅰🍴, map p. 39
🅰 **Municipal** (🛏12, €5): 📷⊙, 📞663324783, ⊙all year, keys at Bar Viñas (looks like regular house, just uphill from the albergue), pleasant secluded location

17.8 Berducedo 🅰 🅷 🍴🛒🍺, see p. 38-39
La Mesa (4.6km farther) is a nice alternate end point if this day feels short.
See accommodations on stage 5, p. 38.

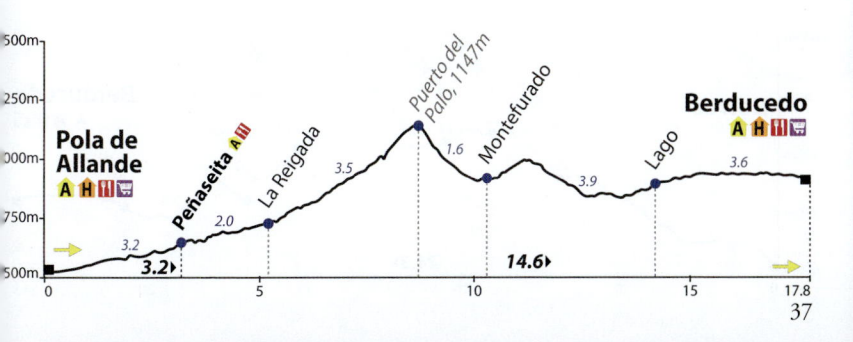

5 BORRES TO BERDUCEDO ❶

24.3km (15.2mi), ⏱ **8-10 Hours**, **Difficulty:** ▬■□
P 5%, 1.1km, U 95%, 23.2km

💡 Walk in the footsteps of pilgrims past as you climb the Sierra Fonfaraón and pass the remains of three historical pilgrim hostels. Enjoy wonderful views in all directions as you climb to the Camino Primitivo's highest elevations, above 1200m (4,000 ft). Rejoin the low route at Puerto del Palo (1147m) and continue through the mountain villages of Montefurado and Lago on your way to Berducedo.

This route across the mountains was the traditional pilgrimage way, passing the remains of three pilgrim *hospitales*: Paradiella (6.8km), Fonfaraón (9.0km), and Valparaiso (10.5km). Hospital de Fonfaraón is the best preserved of the three. After ascending a steep climb after the Hospital de Paradiella, the terrain flattens near a grove of evergreen trees. The flat area and trees make a nice break spot.

The routes rejoin at a pass called Puerto del Palo. From there descend steeply on a dirt path and continue through the abandoned village of Montefurado. Capilla de Montefurado at the entrance of the village was once a pilgrim hospital.

24.3 Berducedo A H 🍴 🛒 🚌

1. **A Municipal** (🛏12, €5): 🚿◯, ☎985929325 (Bar El Cafetín), ⊙all year, keys at Bar El Cafetín, mixed reviews
2. **A H Casa Marqués** (🛏16, €10/20/25-30): 🍴 W D 🛜 ◯, Berducedo 11, ☎985909820, ⊙all year, limited bike space, wifi in bar, individual lockers
3. **A H Camino Primitivo** (🛏19, €12/-/50): 🍴 W D 🛜 ◯, ☎985906670, ⊙Mar-Nov, 🍞 breakfast included in double room price, nice/clean, individual lockers
4. **A H Camin Antiguo** (🛏10, €15/-/60 🍞): 🚿 W D 🛜 ◯, Plaza de la Iglesia, ☎696929164/696929165 📧, ⊙Mar 15-Oct 15, €30 per person in shared double room/€20 per person in shared triple room

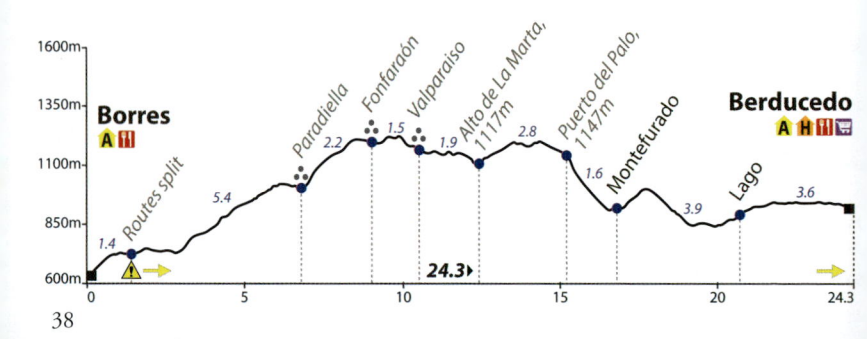

Berducedo
Municipal 1
Cafetín
AS-14
2 Casa Marques
Primitivo 3
4
S. María
Camin Antiguo
100m
Borres
AS-219
0.0
San Pascual
1.4
routes split
Bárcena
El Rebollo
Caborno, 1106m
Stage 5
6.8
Tableiros, 1076m
Hospital de Paradiella
Hospital de Valparaiso
Cimero, 1292m
9.0
10.5
AS-219
Hospital de Fonfaraón
Alto de La Marta, 1117m
La Reigada
(5.2)
Stage 4A: Tineo-Pola de Allande
Peñaseita, +350m
El Caleyo
(3.2)
Santa Coloma
Palo, 1221m
Stage 5A
Pumarín
Puerto del Palo, 1147m
AS-14
(0.0)
Nisón
15.2(8.7)
Panchón, 1411m
routes rejoin
Montefurado
16.8
(10.3)
Pola de Allande
Ablaneda
AS-217
Corondeño
Teijedo
Lago
20.7
(14.2)
Mosqueiro de Fonterro, 1395m
Cereceda
AS-14
Río del Oro
Río de la Pola
AS-14
Prada
Prada
Celón
24.3
(17.8)
Berducedo
Puente Linares
Pumar
Villaverde
N
2 km
0
1
2

6

BERDUCEDO TO GRANDAS DE SALIME

20.7km (12.9mi), ⏱ **6-8 Hours**, Difficulty: ▬▬ ◻ ◼

🅿 54%, 11.1km, Ⓤ 46%, 9.6km

💡 Follow a mix of dirt and paved roads over rolling terrain to La Mesa. After a short climb to a ridgeline with windmills, make a steep, demanding descent to Embalse de Salime (Salime Reservoir). After reaching the dam that forms the reservoir, cross and climb the last 325m up to Grandas de Salime, staying mostly on paved roads with a majestic overlook about halfway up.

4.6 La Mesa A H 🍴

1. A **Municipal** (🛏16, €5): 🚿, ☎985914353, 📅all year, simple
2. A H **Miguelín** (🛏20, €12/-/35): 🍴 W D 🚿 @, ☎985914353 ✉, 📅all year

15.3 Embalse de Salime H 🍴

H **Las Grandas** (€25-35/35-45): 🍴 W D 🚿 @, ☎985627230 ✉, 📅Holy Week-Nov

20.7 Grandas de Salime A H 🍴 🛒 ✚ ℹ 🏧

Grandas de Salime is the largest full-service town in a while. The next grocery stores are in A Fonsagrada (25.7km). Iglesia de San Salvador, in the center of town, was originally constructed in 1186, then completely remodeled in the 17th-19th centuries while retaining its Romanesque front. A 19th-century portico on semicircular arches around the church historically provided shelter to pilgrims. The Museo Etnográfico de Grandas de Salime shows a window into rural Asturian culture (€1.50 ; closed Mondays; free on Tuesdays).

1. A ⭐ **El Salvador** (muni, 🛏28, €6): 🚿 W D 🚿 @, Costa 20, ☎626464183 (Pilar), ☎696221565 (Luis), 📅11:30-10pm all year, clean and well-maintained, nice kitchen
2. A H **Casa Sánchez** (🛏16, €13, apartments €40): 🚿 W D 🚿 @, El Salvador, ☎626665118/985781150 📅Apr 15-Oct 15
3. H **La Barra** (€35/45): 🍴 🚿, Costa 4, ☎985627196/663905284 ✉
4. H **Hostal Occidente** (€25/35): 🍴 W D 🚿, Antonio Machado, ☎659123467
5. H **Pensión A Reigada** (€20/35): 🍴 🚿 @, Pedro de Pedre 9, ☎985627017

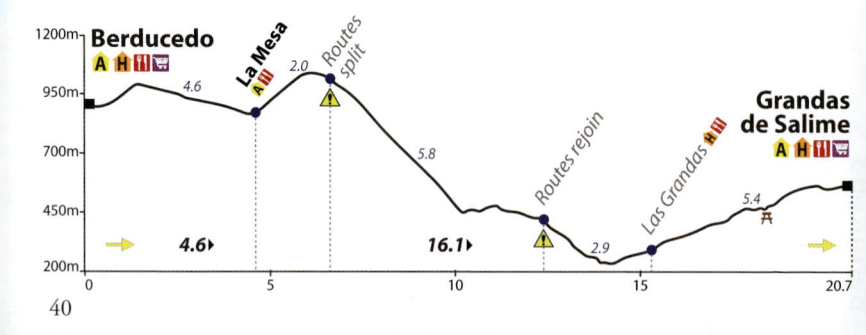

☼ **Due to 2017 forest fires, a provisional detour was created just before Buspol (6.6km).** The detour turns R on a dirt road, while the officialroute continues straight through Buspol, passing the church before descending steeply to the reservoir dam. The main route is shorter and more enjoyable than the detour, though the detour's descent has a more gradual grade.

7
GRANDAS DE SALIME TO A FONSAGRADA

25.7km (16.1mi), ⏱ 7.5-9 Hours, Difficulty: 🟨⬛🟨
P 25%, 6.5km, U 75%, 19.2km

💡 Walk through rural farmland from Grandas de Salime to Castro, with its Bronze Age settlement remains. Ascend to Peñafonte, then continue to climb past ridges lined with windmills, enjoying expansive views along the way. Reach the day's high point (1122m) and bid farewell to Asturias as the path crosses into Galicia with its well-maintained dirt walkways through rolling countryside. Stop for a drink from the cold waters of the fountain in Fonfría!

5.4 Castro A H🍴, cafe in Albergue Juvenil de Castro

The remains of the Bronze Age settlement of Chao Samartín are located just outside town. The settlement dates to the 9th century BCE and remained inhabited until the 2nd century CE. The museum on the south end of town offers guided tours of the archaeological site (Museum: ⏱Tues-Sat 11am-1pm, Sun/holidays 11:30am-1:30pm; guided tours: Tues-Sat 1-5:30pm, Sun/holidays 1:30pm; €2 museum/€4 museum with guided tour)

1. **A Juvenil de Castro** (🛏16, €11): 🔒🍴📶⚡⛺, ☎985924197 📧, ⏱all year except Feb, no youth hostel card required, basic food in cafe but no hot food
2. **H Casa Ferreiro** (€50-80): 🔒🅦📶, ☎679731294 📧, 50m west of Albergue Juvenil de Castro, offers 🍽, small shop with Asturian products
3. **H Hotel Rural Chao San Martín** (€30/40): 🍴⚡, Aldea Castro 1A, ☎985627267

25.7 A Fonsagrada A H🍴🏪➕€ℹ️📮

A Fonsagrada is named after its *fons sacrata* (sacred fountain), located just behind Iglesia de Santa María. According to legend, St. James was cared for by a poor widow in the town. Out of gratitude for her help, he turned water from the village fountain into milk.

1. **A Ramón Rodríguez** (Xunta, 🛏42, €6): 🔒⚡, San Roque 4, ☎699776572, ⏱1pm all year, well maintained in beautiful renovated building; few cooking utensils in kitchen
2. **A H Cantábrico** (🛏34, €10/30/50): 🔒🅦📶⚡, Fonte, ☎669747560 📧, ⏱all year
3. **A Os Chaos** (🛏22, €10): 🔒🅦🅓📶⚡, Marmoiral 26, ☎630347224, ⏱Easter-Oct
4. **H Casa Manolo** (€25-30/35-40): 🍴🅦🅓📶⚡, Burón 35, ☎982340408 📧
5. **A H O Piñeiral** (🛏44, €10/30/50): 🔒🍴🅦🅓📶⚡, LU-530 km 3.9, ☎982340350, 606165752 📧, ⏱all year, +3.2km past A Fonsagrada (see stage 8 map)

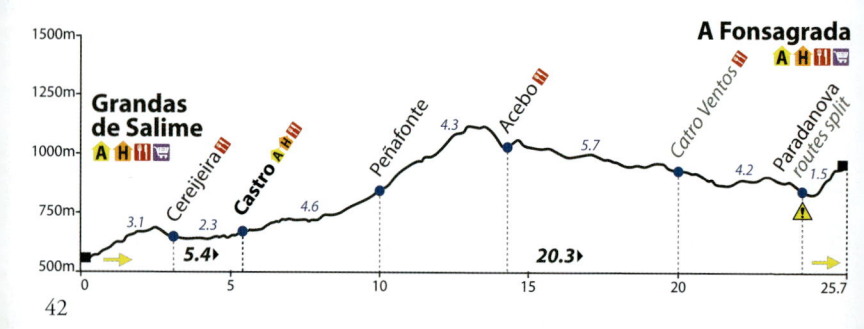

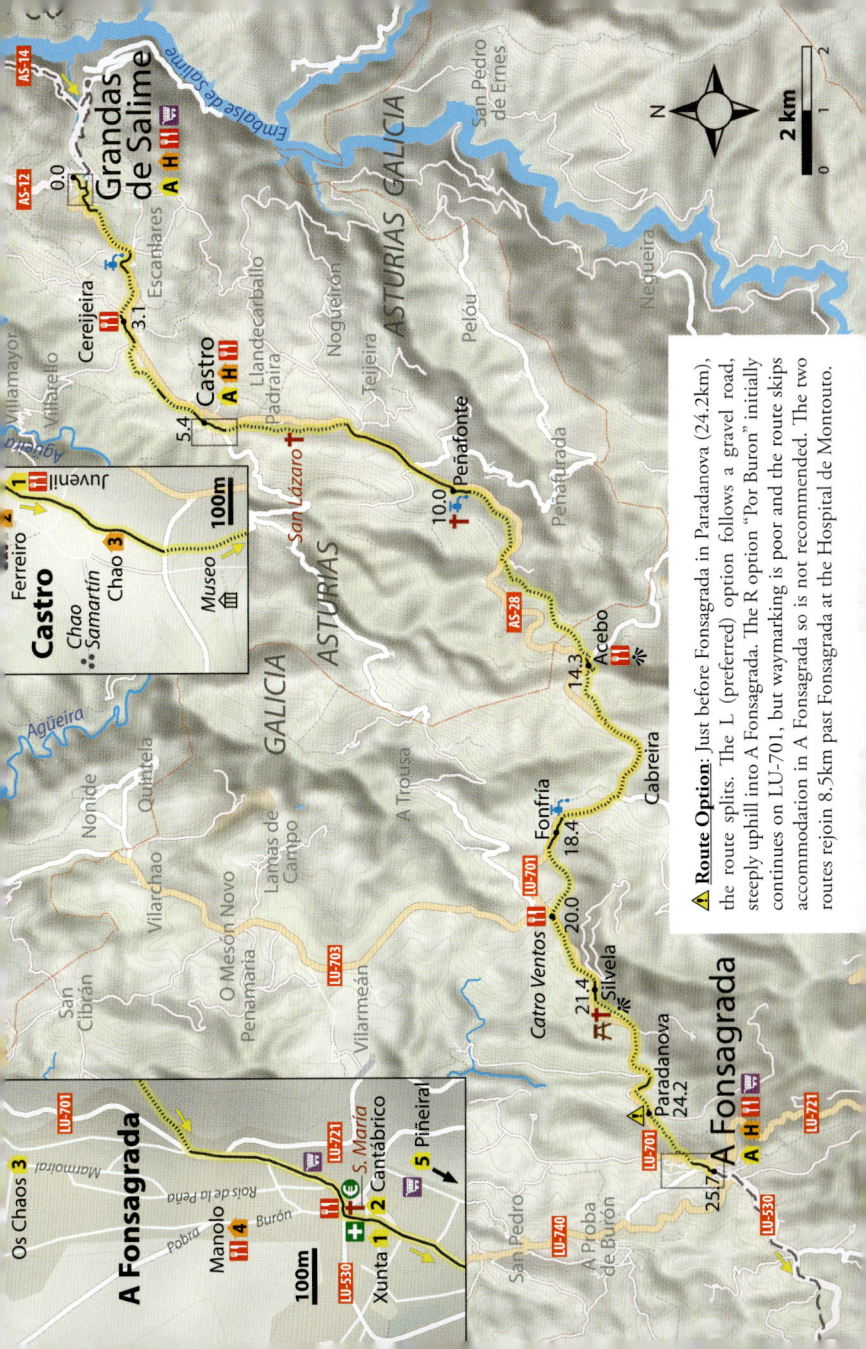

⚠ **Route Option:** Just before Fonsagrada in Paradanova (24.2km), the route splits. The L (preferred) option follows a gravel road, steeply uphill into A Fonsagrada. The R option "Por Buron" initially continues on LU-701, but waymarking is poor and the route skips accommodation in A Fonsagrada so is not recommended. The two routes rejoin 8.5km past Fonsagrada at the Hospital de Montouto.

8

A FONSAGRADA TO O CÁDAVO

24.3km (15.2mi), ⏱ **7-9 Hours**, **Difficulty:** 🟧🟧⬜
🅿 24%, 5.7km, Ⓤ 76%, 18.6km

💡 Enjoy the last day in the higher mountains on the Camino Primitivo. The day's walk follows a mix of mostly dirt roads and narrow dirt paths through a number of rural Galician villages that dot the mountainous terrain. After the first climb of the day, reach the Hospital de Montouto. After a descent, the bar in Paradavella is a good spot to take a rest—some steep climbs await ahead. Once reaching Alto de Fontaneira, it's mostly downhill to O Cádavo.

The Hospital de Montouto was founded by Peter the Cruel in 1360 and continued to host pilgrims into the 20th century. A chapel is located at the site, and a few dolmens are situated behind the hospital.

24.3 O Cádavo 🅰🅷🛒➕€🚌

If you'd prefer a shorter walk into Lugo on the following day, consider continuing onward to Castroverde (an additional 8km).

1. 🅰 **Xunta** (🛏22, €6): 🅺 📶⊙, Feira, ☎636947117, ⏱1-10pm all year, small, clean and simple, few outlets
2. 🅰 **San Mateo** (🛏44, €10): 🅺🍴🅦🅓 📶⊙, Feira 2, ☎616529514, ⏱11am Apr-Oct, coffee/snack vending machines, individual lockers
3. 🅰🅷 **Porta Santa** (🛏8, €11/30/40): 🅺🅦🅓 📶⊙, Escobar 9, ☎679828540, ⏱11am-10pm all year, coffee/snack vending machines
4. 🅷 **Pensión Eligio** (€20/35): 🍴🅦🅓 📶⊙, Feira, ☎982354009, adjacent to/same owner as Albergue San Mateo
5. 🅷 **Moneda** (€26/43): 🍴🅦🅓 📶⊙, Baralla 46, ☎982354001/982355205, restaurant with menú del día

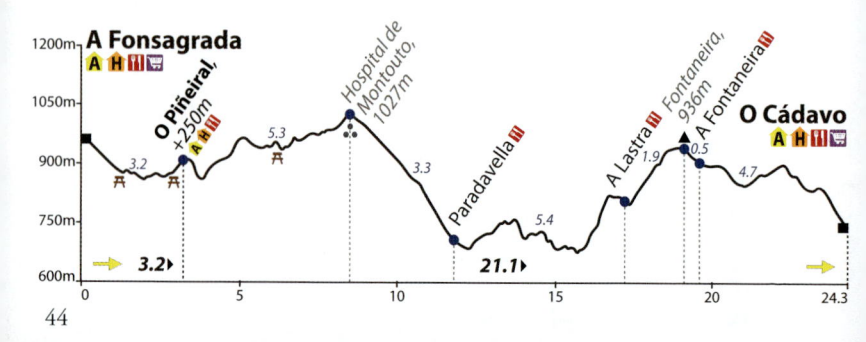

A Fonsagrada

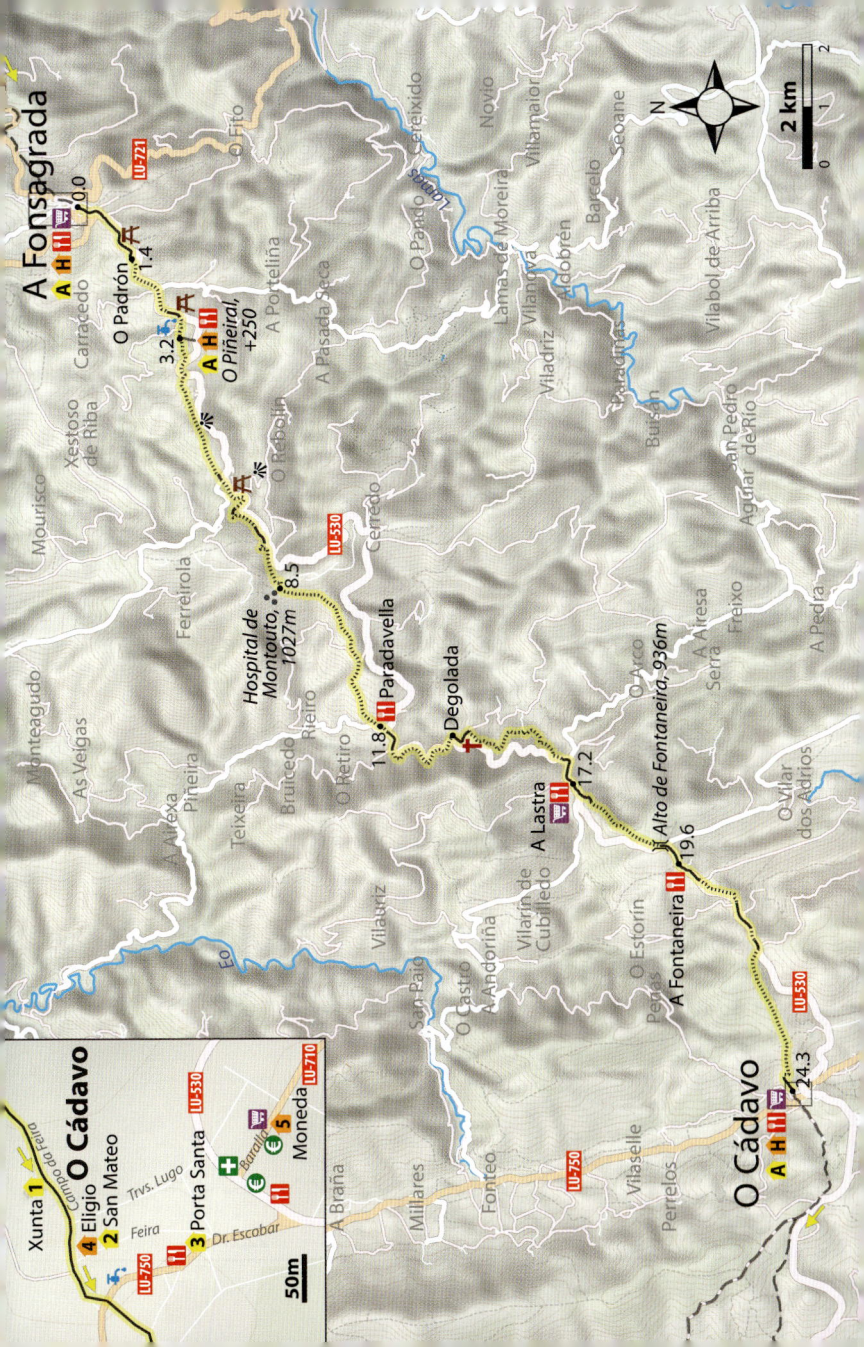

LU-221

0.0 A H ⊤⊤

Carracedo
O Padrón 1.4 ⊤⊤
Xestoso de Riba
                  3.2 A H ⊤⊤
                  O Piñeiral, +250
Mourisco   O Rebolin   A Pasada Seca
          Ferreirola   A Portelina
                                              Lamas de Moreira
                                              Vilanova
                                              Vilamaior   Vilobol de Arriba
                                              Idobrén
                  LU-530
                  8.5
As Veigas   Cereixedo
          A Aulfexa   Viladriz
                  Pineira
                  Teixeira   11.8 ⊤⊤ Paradavella   Buxán
          Monteagudo Bruicedo   San Pedro
                  O Retiro   Aguar de Río
                          Rieiro   A Pedra
                                  Degolada
                                  ✝
                          Vilauriz   Ozcoo
                                          17.2 A Lastra ⊤⊤   A Airesa
                                                              Serra
                                          19.6 Alto de Fontaneira, 936m Freixo O Vilar dos Adrios
                  San Pai
                          Vilarín de   O Estorín
                          Cubilledo   O Castro
                                  Andoriña   Pazos   A Fontaneira ⊤⊤
                                                              O Cádavo
                                                              24.3
                                          A Braña   A H ⊤⊤
                                                  Fonteo Vilaselle
                                                  LU-750
                                                          Millares   Perrelos

O Cádavo (inset)

LU-710

1 Xunta
4 Eligio
2 San Mateo
3 Porta Santa
5 Moneda

Campo da Feira
Trvs. Lugo
Feira
Baralla
Dr. Escobar

LU-530
LU-750

50m

2 km

O CÁDAVO TO LUGO

9

30.2km (18.9mi), ⏱ 8-11 Hours, Difficulty: ▬ ▮ ▮
P 50%, 15.2km, U 50%, 15.0km

💡 After a manageable climb out of O Cádavo, descend to Vilabade and visit the town's Gothic church before continuing to Castroverde. After Castroverde, you'll encounter few services as you pass through rural farmland and agricultural villages on your way to Lugo. A well-supplied vending machine in a roofed enclosure in Gondar makes a good rest stop around halfway through the day. Lugo is a welcome reward after a long day's walk. The city has some wonderful sites, and impressive large Roman walls encircle the old city.

⚠ **Route Option**: At the top of the climb from Cádavo, the route splits at a Y intersection:
1) The first (preferred) route continues straight on a dirt road along the hillside, before reaching a paved road and turning L, passing the Capela de Carme and a shaded picnic area before descending into Vilabade.
2) The second option (600m shorter) follows the L fork and descends through Vilalle before joining the first route in Castroverde.

6.2 Vilabade H 🍴
There is a mobile food stand at the entrance to town in summer. A Franciscan community existed in Vilabade dating to the 15th century, and the town was a major stopping point for pilgrims. The Iglesia de Santa María, also known as the "Catedral de Castroverde," was built in 1457. The church is a national monument and a splendid example of 15th-century Gothic architecture. Across the church courtyard is the Pazo de Vilabade, a manor house built for Diego Osorio Escobar (Bishop and Viceroy of New Spain).
H **Pazo de Vilabade** (€140/190): 🍴 W D 🅿 🛜 ◉, ☏615905554 ✉, ⏱all year, the hotel requires that a total of 5 rooms be booked to open outside of July/August

8.0 Castroverde A H 🍴 🛒 ✚ 🚌
1. A **Xunta** (🛏34, €6): 🎒 🛜 ◉, ☏699832747, 638778353, ⏱1-10pm all year, limited utensils in kitchen
2. H **Pensión Cortés** (€20/38): 🍴 🛜 ◉, Feira 15, ☏982312166

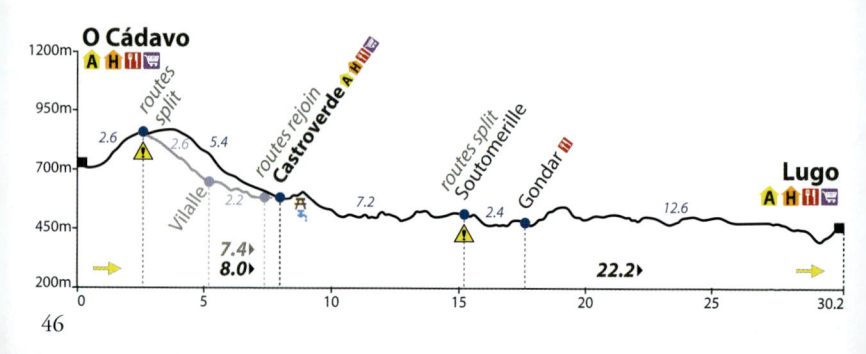

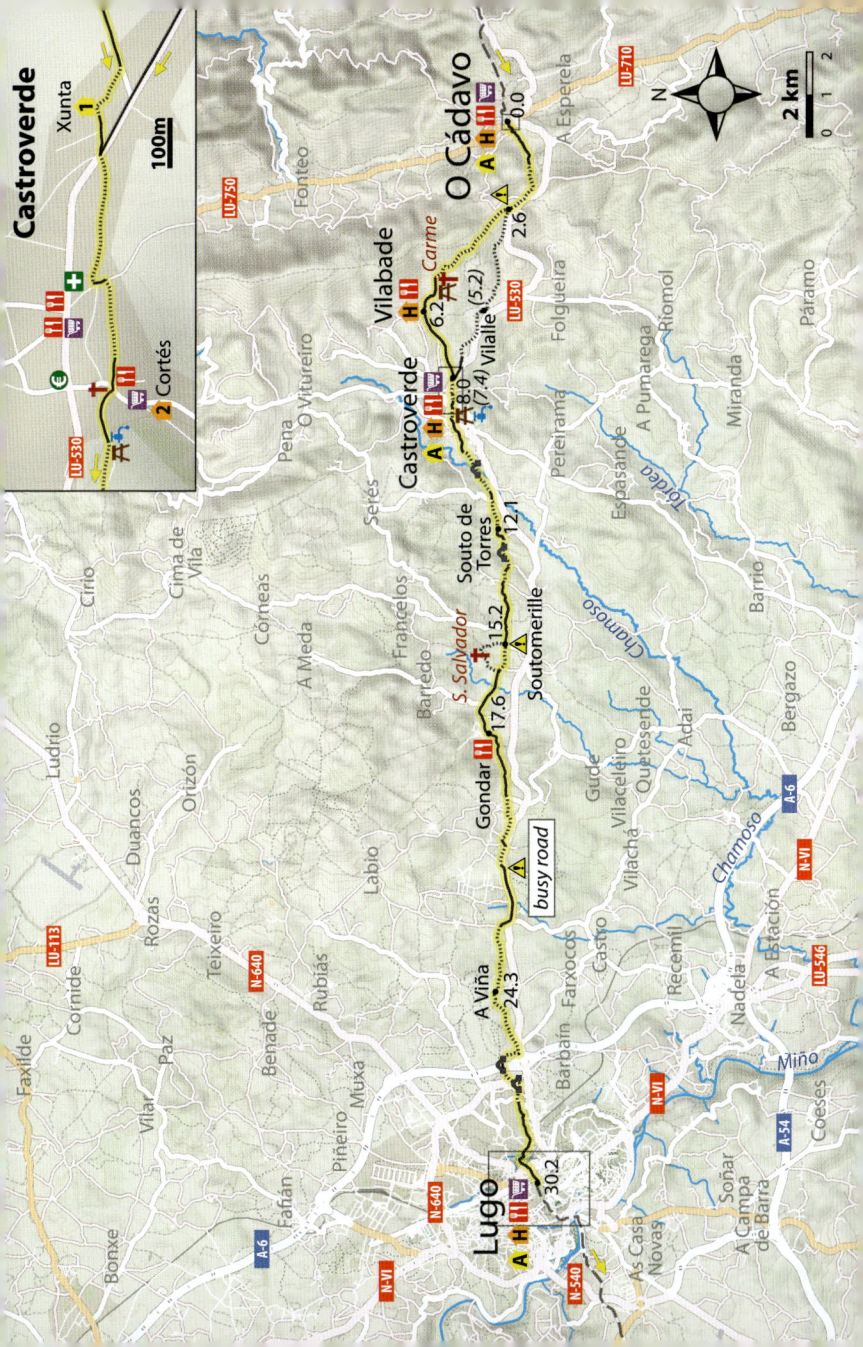

Castroverde

Xunta

1

100m

2 Cortés

LU-530

O Cádavo 0.0
A H ¶¶
2.6
LU-710
A Esperela
LU-750
Fonteo
Vilabade 6.2 *Carme*
H ¶¶
(5.2)
LU-530
(7.4) Vilalle
Folgueira
Ritmol
Páramo
Castroverde 8.0
A H ¶¶
Pereirama
A Pumarega
Miranda
Souto de Torres 12.1
Soutomerille
S. Salvador 15.2
17.6 Gondar ¶¶
Chamoso (Chamoso)
Quesoserde
Adai
Bergazo
Barrio
Tórdea
Espasande

busy road

A Viña 24.3
LU-113
N-640
Rubiás
Castro
Farxocos
Recemil
A Estación
A-6
N-VI
LU-546
Nadela

Lugo 30.2
A H ¶¶
N-VI
A-54
N-540
As Casa Novas
A Campa de Barra
Sonar
Coeses
Miño

N ↑ 2 km 0 1 2

Camino Primitivo

30.2 Lugo

Lugo is 100km from Santiago. Be sure to get two stamps per day from here until Santiago! Lugo was likely founded by Celtic inhabitants of the region, who dedicated the town to Lugos, the Celtic god of light. In 13BCE the city was conquered by the Romans, who ruled until the 5th century CE. Later the town was ceded to the Suebi and Visigoths. After a period of decline, the city rebounded and was a center of pilgrimage in the Middle Ages.

Today Lugo is the only city in the world to be entirely surrounded by intact Roman walls. The wall around the city stands between 8-12m high and 4-7m thick. There are 10 gates and 71 towers. It's possible to completely circumnavigate the city along the top of the wall (2.1km). Other notable Roman remains include the Roman bridge over the Río Miño, Roman baths (in Hotel Balneario), and the Mosaics House. Construction on the impressive Catedral de Santa María began in 1129 in Romanesque style and later incorporated Romanesque, Gothic, Baroque, and Neoclassical elements. The Convento de San Francisco houses the Museo Provincial, which has displays of Galician art. The Festival de San Froilán (Oct 4-12) commemorates the city's patron saint. During the festival, it's popular to eat octopus from stands near Rosalía Castro Park. Arde Lucus, celebrated in the last weeks of June, celebrates the Roman and Celtic past of the city.

1. **Xunta** (44, €6): Noreas, 618425578, 1-10pm all year, kitchen has only a few utensils
2. **Casa Chanca** (13, €15): 12pm Holy Week-Nov, good reviews, bike storage in garden (not inside)
3. **Shiku Hostel** (12, €15/-/32): Noreas 2, 982229935, all year, 24-hour reception
4. **Hostel Cross** (24, €14-15): Cruz 14, 604026605
5. **Lucus** (8, €19/25/38): Rei Don García 1, 608072819
6. **Juvenil Lug2** (youth hostel, 16, €9/17+/25+): Pintor Corredoira 4, 982828492, 4pm all year
7. **Roots and Boots** (27, €12/-/25): Santiago 214, 982229709, 12-10pm, mixed reviews
8. **Ciudad de Lugo** (€40+): Carril das Hortas 29, 982284707, rooms with kitchens for 2-3 people, self-service laundry closeby
9. **Méndez Núñez** (€65+): Raiña 1, 982230711
10. **Monumento Pazo de Orbán** (€110+): Miño 6, 982240217
11. **Pensión San Roque** (€24-28/30-38): Mártires Carral 11, 982222700
12. **Exe Puerta San Pedro** (€45+): Río Neira 29, 982222381
13. **España** (€25/35): Vilalba 2, 982816062
14. **Muralla Romana (B&B)** (€27+/34+): Cidade de Viveiro 5, 667734859/982804522
15. **Gran Hotel Lugo** (€60+): Ramón Ferreiro 21, 982224152
16. **Metropol** (€33+/40): Miguel de Cervantes 58, 982813597
17. **Apartamento de María** (€50+/55+): Conde 20, 637223216, Apartment with capacity for 6 people (+€5 for each additional person)
18. **Apartamento Avenida Coruña 32** (€45+): Coruña 32, 653821841, Apartment with capacity for 6 people (+€7 for each additional person)

Lugo

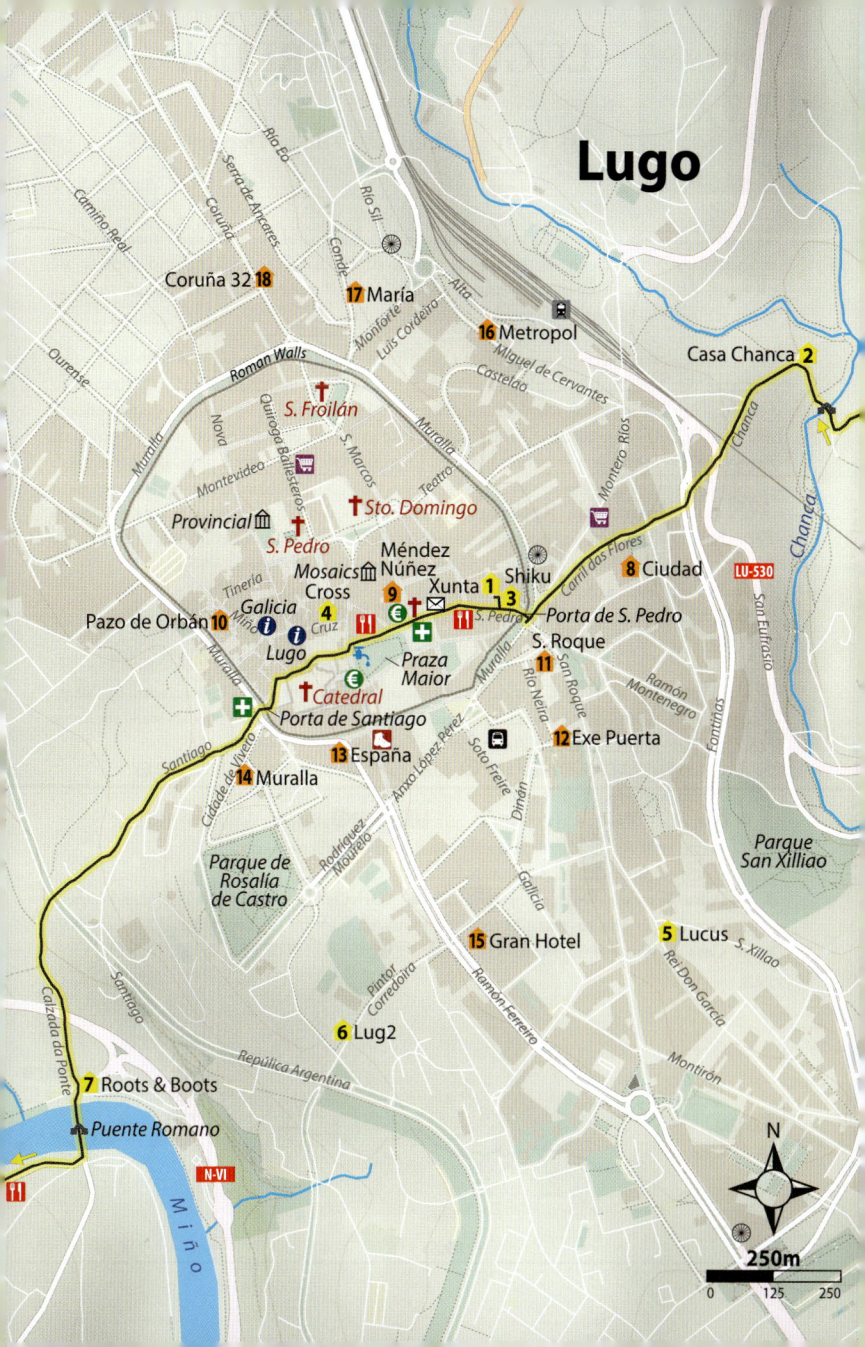

- Casa Chanca **2**
- Coruña 32 **18**
- María **17**
- Metropol **16**
- Roman Walls
- S. Froilán
- Sto. Domingo
- Provincial
- S. Pedro
- Mosaics
- Méndez Núñez
- Cross
- Shiku
- Xunta **1 3**
- Galicia **4**
- Ciudad **8**
- Pazo de Orbán **10**
- Cruz **9**
- Lugo
- Porta de S. Pedro
- S. Roque **11**
- Praza Maior
- Catedral
- Porta de Santiago
- España **13**
- Exe Puerta **12**
- Muralla **14**
- Parque de Rosalía de Castro
- Parque San Xilliao
- Gran Hotel **15**
- Lucus **5**
- Lug2 **6**
- Roots & Boots **7**
- Puente Romano

250m

10

LUGO TO FERREIRA

26.1km (16.3mi), ⏱ **7-9 Hours**, Difficulty: ▣▣▢
▣ 72%, 18.9km, ▣ 28%, 7.2km

💡 Leave Lugo via the Roman bridge over the Río Miño and continue into rural Galician countryside. While much of the day is on paved surfaces, the walking and scenery are pleasant. After San Román da Retorta, enjoy a few kilometers on unpaved dirt roads to approach Ferreira, a small village with a Roman bridge.

The number of walkers increases after Lugo (final 100km to Santiago), and beds can be scarce before Melide. If you plan to stay in private albergues in San Román da Retorta or Ferreira, consider reserving your bed ahead of time. There are few services other than a vending machine and off-route café in O Burgo and a café at Albergue O Cándido in San Román da Retorta. There are no grocery stores between Lugo and Melide, so stock up in Lugo if needed.

19.5 **San Román da Retorta** A H ¶ Pass the Iglesia de Santa Cruz da Retorta, a 12th-century Romanesque church, as you enter this small town and continue an additional 800m, crossing LU-P-1611 to reach the private and Xunta albergues.
1. **A Xunta** (🛏12, €6): ▣◉, ☏628173456, ⏱1-10pm ⏱all year
2. **A H O Cándido** (🛏20, €10/20/30 ▣): ¶ W D 📶◉, ☏693063146 ✉, ⏱Apr-Oct, mixed reviews

26.1 **Ferreira** A H ¶ Consider walking another 6.3km to As Seixas with its Xunta albergue in a beautifully-restored stone building. From As Seixas, you can walk to Arzúa (28.7km), leaving yourself two 20km days to Santiago.
1. **A Cruz** (🛏18, €10): ▣¶ W D 📶◉, Mámoa 9, ☏982178908/618597822 ✉,
   ⏱1-10pm Apr-Sep, slightly off-route before Ferreira but well signed
2. **A H A Nave** (🛏40, €11/35-40/40-50): ¶ W D 📶◉, Covela, ☏616161594 ✉,
   ⏱1-10pm mid Apr-mid Nov, breakfast included for private rooms,
   clean/professional with nice common area, vegetarian/vegan dinner option
3. **A Ponte Ferreira** (🛏22, €11): ¶ W D 📶◉, Carballal 2, ☏982036949 ✉, ⏱1-10pm
   Jun-Nov (varies year-to-year), in renovated Galician farmhouse, vegetarian dinner option
4. **H Casa da Ponte** (€30-35/40-45): ¶ W D 📶◉, ☏982183077 ✉, ⏱mid Mar-Oct

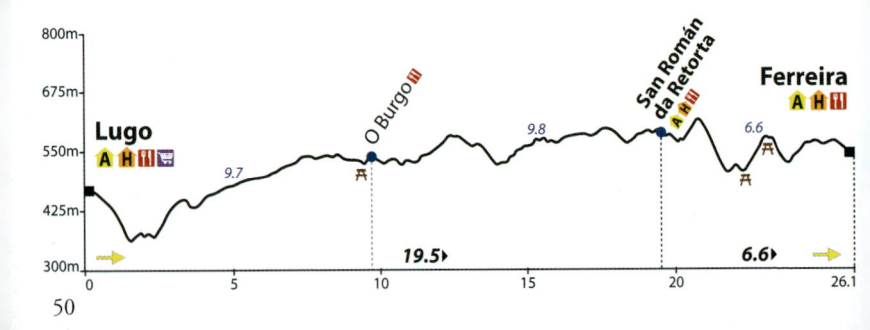

Lugo

- 0.0 Lugo
- 7.5 Vilastévez / Seoane / Fonte Ribicás
- 9.7 O Burgo
- 13.4 Bacurín / Hospital
- 19.5 San Pedro de Baixo / San Román da Retorta
- 26.1 Ferreira (+6.3 km to As Seixas)

San Román da Retorta

- Sta. Cruz da Retorta
- O Cándido
- Xunta 1

Ferreira

- Cruz 1
- Cantina / A Nave 2
- Puente Romano / Ponte 3
- Casa da Ponte 4

11

FERREIRA TO MELIDE

21.1km (13.2mi), ⏱ 5-7 Hours, Difficulty: ▰▢▢
🅿 69%, 14.6km, Ⓤ 31%, 6.5km

💡 Enjoy a day of tranquility before the crowds in Melide, where the Camino Francés and Primitivo join for the last 53km to Santiago. Climb a moderate pass and continue on dirt roads through Vilouriz to Vilamor. The last 7km to Melide are a bit uninspiring, but they pass quickly. In Melide, try *Pulpo Gallego* (octopus specialty) at Pulpería Ezequiel!

6.3 As Seixas 🅰 🍴
A small bar serves meals, but notify them in advance. A vending machine outside the albergue sells basic food items—enough for a meal in a pinch.
🅰 ⭐ **Xunta** (🛏35, €6): 🛏🚻🍳📶🔌, 📞609669057, 🕐1-10pm all year

7.7 Casacamiño 🅷
🅷 **Casa Camiño** (€60-85): 🍴🚻🍳📶🔌, Casacamiño 4, 📞982036946, good reviews

21.1 Melide 🅰🅷🍴🛒➕ℹ🏧

1. 🅰 **Xunta** (🛏156, €6): 🛏🚻🍳, San Antonio, 📞660396822, 🕐1pm all year, no cookware
2. 🅰 **O Apalpador** (🛏30, €10): 🛏🚻🍳🛒, San Antonio 23, 📞679837969, 🕐all year
3. 🅰 **San Antón** (🛏36, €10-12): 🍴🛏🚻🍳🛒📶, Antonio 6, 📞981506427, 🕐Mar-Oct
4. 🅰🅷 **Vilela** (🛏24, €10/25/30): 🛏🚻🍳📶, San Antonio 2, 📞616011375, 🕐all year
5. 🅰🅷 **Candil** (🛏12, €15/-/45-65 🛏): 🍴🛏🚻🍳📶🔌, Principal 21, 📞639503550, 🕐12pm Mar-Oct
6. 🅰🅷 **Pereiro** (🛏45, €10/30/40): 🛏🚻🍳📶🔌, Progreso 43, 📞981506314, 🕐a. y.
7. 🅰 **Alfonso II El Casto** (🛏35, €12): 🛏🚻🍳📶🔌, Ac. Toques Friol 52, 📞981506454
8. 🅰 **O Cruceiro** (🛏72, €10): 🛏🚻🍳🛒📶, Coruña 2, 📞616764896, 🕐Mar-Oct
9. 🅰 **Arraigos** (🛏20, €8-10): 🛏🚻🍳🛒📶, S. Roque 9, 📞600880769, 🕐all year
10. 🅰🅷 **Montoto** (🛏40, €12/-/30): 🛏🚻🍳📶, Codeseira 31, 📞646941887
11. 🅰 **Melide** (🛏42, €10-12): 🚻🍳📶, Lugo 92, 📞627901552, 🕐Easter-Oct, lockers
12. 🅷 **Chiquitin** (€35/50): 🍴📶, San Antonio 18, 📞981815333
13. 🅷 **Pensión Berenguela** (€30/45): 📶, San Roque 2, 📞981505417
14. 🅷 **Hotel Xaneiro** (€35/45): 🍴📶, Habana 43, 📞981506140
15. 🅷 **Hotel Carlos 96**: (€50): 🍴📶, Lugo 119, 📞981507633
16. 🅷 **Hospedaje Bar Sony** (€28/37): 🍴📶, Cedeseira, 📞981506473

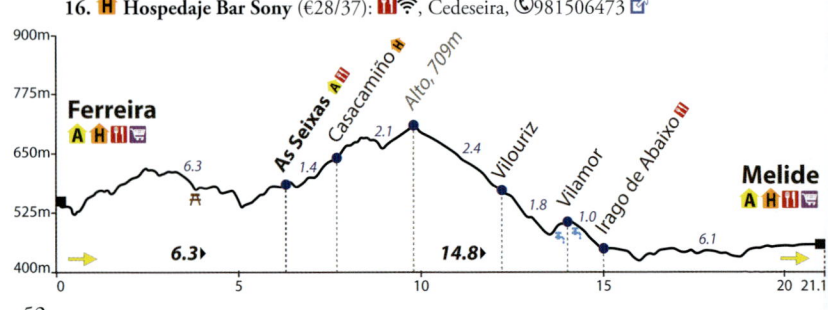

Ferreira

0.0

As Seixas
6.3

Hostpial das Seixas
7.7

Casacamiño

Alto, 709m

Viloüriz

12.2

Vilamor
14.0

Irago de Abaixo
15.0

Melide
21.1

As Seixas
Xunta 1

Melide

Sancti Spíritus
Terra de Melide
S. Antón Vilela
Chiquitín 12 3 4
Xunta 1 2 5 El Candil
O Apalpador 6 Pereiro
Sony
16 Montoto
progreso

7 Alfonso II
San António
8 Berenguela
13
Parque 9 Arraigos
Lugo Melide
14 Xaneiro
S. Roque
Carlos 96 15
Ezequiel
11
Martín Freire
El Crucero
Coruña

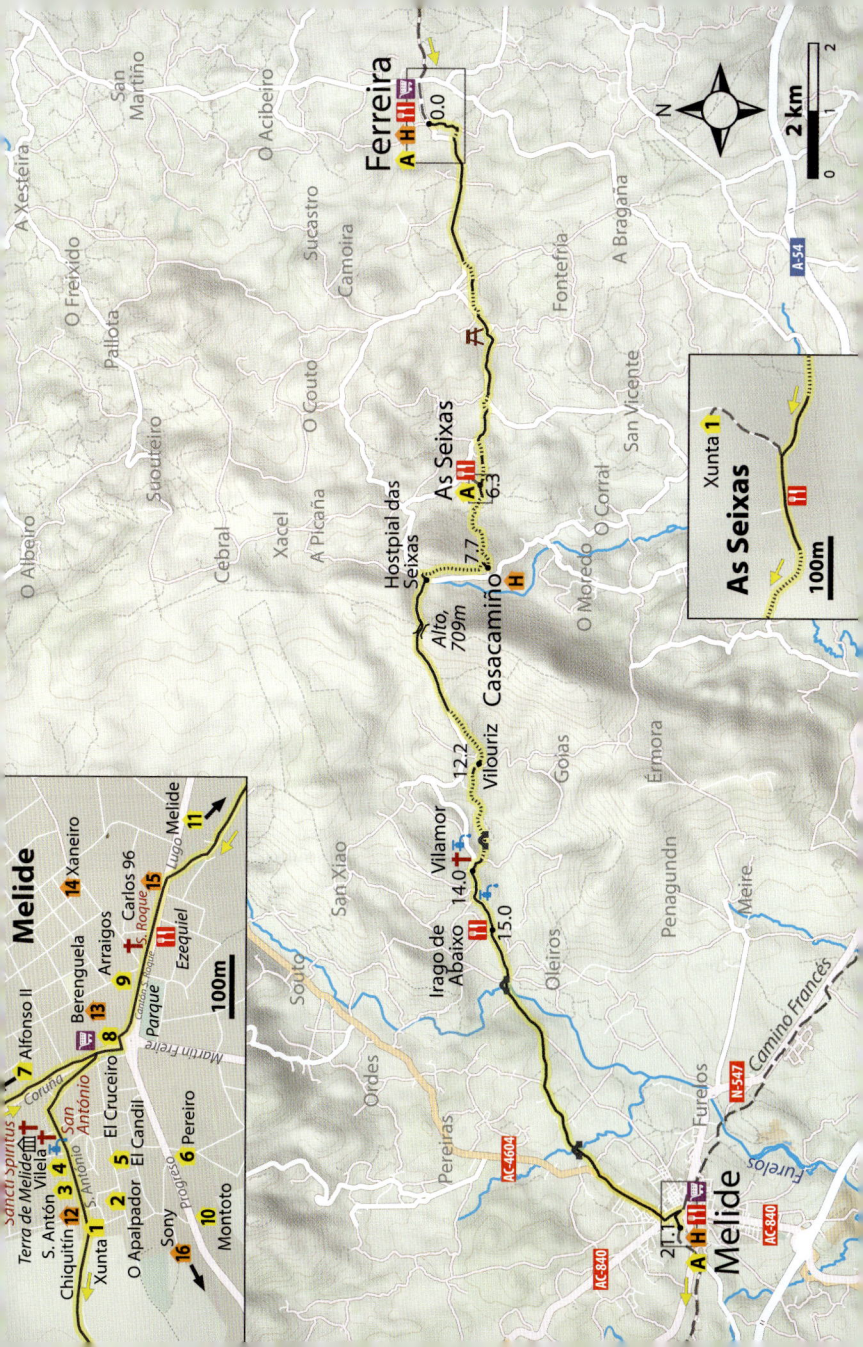

12 MELIDE TO ARCA

33.0km (20.6mi), ⏱ **9-12 Hours**, Difficulty: ▬▬■■
🅿 30%, 10.0km, Ⓤ 70%, 23.0km

💡 A long stage with constant ups and downs through small villages and the larger pilgrim town of Arzúa. Fragrant eucalyptus groves provide plenty of shade. Shortly after Melide, pass Iglesia de Santa María, a 12th-century Romanesque church with notable 15th-century frescoes including a depiction of the trinity surrounded by the four evangelists and twelve apostles. Just after the church, a small bridge spans the Río Lázaro. There is a small house here, originally the chapel of San Lázaro, where the Iglesia de Santa María operated a leprosarium.

5.5 Boente A H 🍴🚌
This village features the 20th-century Iglesia de Santiago incorporating earlier elements and has both a Santiago Peregrino and Matamoros. A fountain known as the *Fonte da Saleta* is said to have curative powers, located next to a stone *rollo* or roadside cross. Boente's streets underwent major renovations in 2011, now in tip-top shape.
- **A H Boente** (⛺54, €10-12/35/40): 🍴Ⓦ🄳📶🍽, ☎981501974, ⊙Mar-Nov
- **A Os Albergues** (⛺30, €11): Ⓦ🄳📶, ☎981501853, ⊙Mar-Oct

7.8 Castañeda A H 🍴🚌
Castañeda was the destination of the limestone that medieval pilgrims carried from Triacastela to be finished in the ovens and used in constructing the cathedral. The town must have been a welcome site! Nothing remains of the ovens, which are mentioned in the *Codex Calixtinus*.
- **A H Santiago** (⛺4, €11/-/35): 🍴Ⓦ🄳📶, ☎981501711, ⊙call in winter
- **H Casa Rural Milia** (€45/60): 🍴📶, Lugar Portela, ☎981501625

10.8 Ribadiso da Baixo A H 🍴🚌
The location of the bridge dates to the 6th century. The pilgrim hospital of San Antón served pilgrims in the 16th century and was restored in 1993 to return to use as a Xunta albergue.
- **A Xunta** (⛺70, €6): 🄺Ⓦ🄳📶, ☎981501185, ⊙1pm all year, no cookware, restored historic buildings along the river
- **A H Los Caminantes** (⛺56, €10/-/35-40): 🄺Ⓦ🄳📶, ☎647020600, ⊙Apr-Oct
- **A Milpés** (⛺24, €10): 🍴Ⓦ🄳📶, Ribadiso 7, ☎981500425

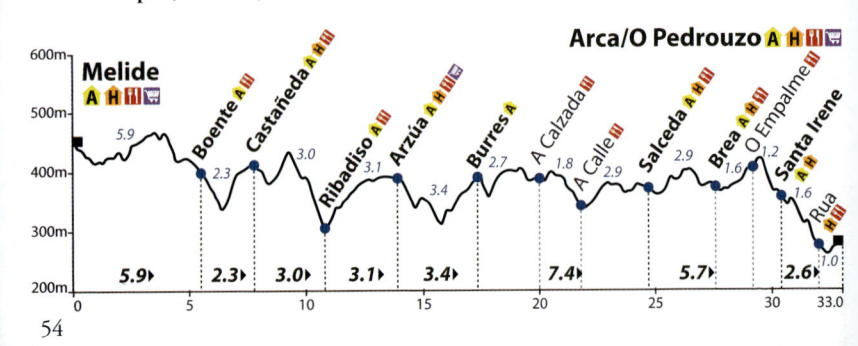

Arzúa

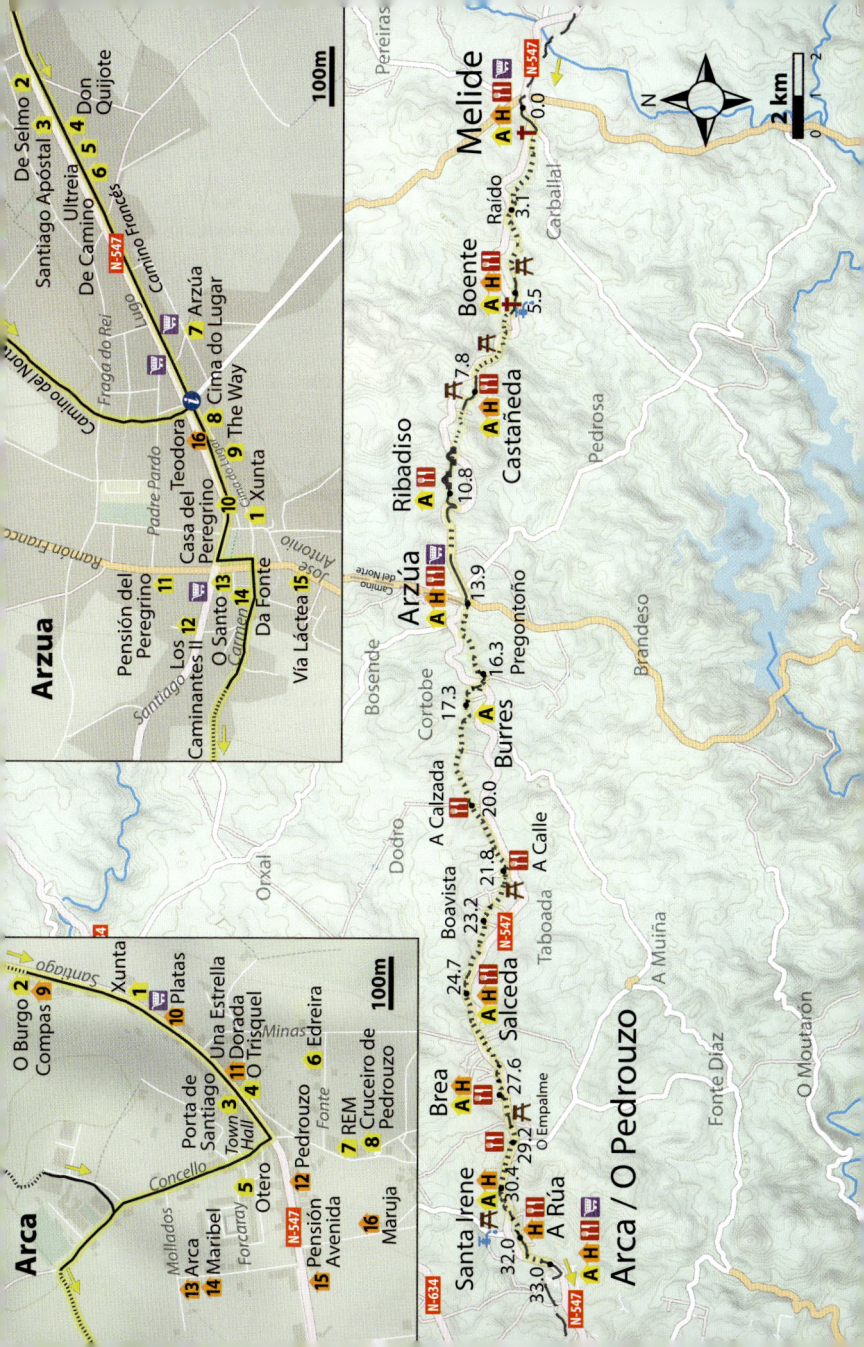

- Santiago Apóstol **3** De Selmo **2**
- Ultreia De Camino **6** Don Quijote **4**
- **5** Camino Francés
- **7** Arzúa
- **8** Cima do Lugar
- **16** **i**
- **9** The Way
- **10** Casa del Peregrino
- **1** Xunta
- **11** Pensión del Peregrino
- **12** Los Caminantes II
- **13** O Santo
- **14** Da Fonte Carmen
- **15** Vía Láctea

Arca

- O Burgo **2** Compas **9**
- **1** Xunta
- **10** Platas
- **3** Porta de Santiago Una Estrella **11**
- **4** O Trisquel Dorada
- **5** Otero
- **6** Edreira
- **12** Pedrouzo
- **7** REM
- **8** Cruceiro de Pedrouzo
- **13** Arca
- **14** Maribel
- **15** Pensión Avenida
- **16** Maruja

Melide 0.0
Raído 3.1
Boente 5.5
7.8
Castañeda
Ribadiso 10.8
Arzúa 13.9
Pregontoño 16.3
Burres 17.3
Cortobe
A Calzada 20.0
A Calle 21.8
Boavista 23.2
24.7
Salceda
Brea 27.6
29.2 O Empalme
Santa Irene 30.4
A Rúa 32.0
33.0
Arca / O Pedrouzo

13.9 Arzúa 🅰 🅷 🍴🛒✚€ℹ️🚌

Arzúa was previously known as Villanova, as it is called in the Codex Calixtinus. Two pilgrim hospices were located here. The Iglesia de Santiago is a 20th-century structure with a 19th-century retablo depicting the battle of Clavijo and Santiago Matamoros' appearance. The town is famous for its delicious creamy cheese. The central plaza features a statue of a cheesemaker, and an annual March cheese festival sells over 100,000 cheeses each year. This was the traditional stopping point before Santiago for medieval pilgrims.

1. 🅰 **Xunta** (🛏48, €6): 🅺🆆🅳, Cima Lugar 6, ☎660396824, 🕐1pm all year, no cookware
2. 🅰 **De Selmo** (🛏50, €10-12): 🅺🆆🅳📶, Lugo 133, ☎981939018 ✉
3. 🅰 **Santiago Apóstol** (🛏72, €10-12): 🅺🆆🅳📶, Lugo 107, ☎981508132 ✉, 🕐all year
4. 🅰 🅷 **Don Quijote** (🛏50, €10 €35/45): 🅺🆆🅳📶◉, Lugo 130, ☎981500139 ✉, 🕐all year
5. 🅰 **Ultreia** (🛏39, €10): 🍴🅺🆆🅳📶◉, Lugo 126, ☎981500471 ✉, 🕐all year
6. 🅰 **De Camino** (🛏46, €10-12): 🆆🅳📶, Lugo 118, ☎981500415 ✉, 🕐Mar-Nov
7. 🅰 🅷 **Arzúa** (🛏12, €10/-/30-40): 🅺🆆🅳📶, Rosa. Castro 2, ☎981508233, Feb-Nov
8. 🅰 **Cima do Lugar** (🛏14, €10/37/47): 🆆🅳📶, Cima do Lugar 22, ☎981500559 ✉, 🕐all year
9. 🅰 **The Way** (🛏40, €10-17): 🍴🆆🅳📶, Cima Lugar 28, ☎604051353 ✉, 🕐Apr-Nov
10. 🅰 **Casa del Peregrino** (🛏14, €10-12): 🅺🆆🅳📶, Cima do Lugar 7, ☎686708704 ✉
11. 🅰 🅷 **Pensión del Peregrino** (€15/36/50): 🍴📶, Ramón Franco 7, ☎981500145 ✉
12. 🅰 **Caminantes II** (🛏28, €10): 🅺🆆🅳📶, Sant. 14, ☎647020600 ✉, 🕐Apr-Oct
13. 🅰 **Santo** (🛏22, €12/36/-): 🅺🆆🅳📶◉, Xosé Vilas 4, ☎981500957 ✉, 🕐Apr-Oct
14. 🅰 **Da Fonte** (🛏20, €10-12): 🅺🆆🅳📶, Carmen 18, ☎604002380 ✉, 🕐Mar-Oct
15. 🅰 **Vía Láctea** (🛏60, €10-12): 🅺🆆🅳📶, José N. Vilas 26, ☎981500581 ✉, 🕐a. y.
16. 🅷 **Hostal Teodora** (€38/48): 🅳📶, Lugo 38, ☎981500083 ✉

17.3 Burres 🅰 🛒

🅰 **Camiño das Ocas** (🛏30, €12): 🅺🆆🅳📶, ☎648404780 ✉, 🕐all year, +400m

24.7 Salceda 🅰 🅷 🍴🚌

Soon after Salceda, note the memorial to Guillermo Watt (25.6km), a pilgrim who died here in 1993 just one day shy of Santiago.

🅰 **Boni** (🛏20, €12): 🅺🆆🅳📶, ☎618965907 ✉, 🕐Mar-Oct
🅰 🅷 **Alborada** (🛏10, €12/-/50): 🅺🆆🅳📶, ☎981502956 ✉, 🕐Apr-Oct
🅰 🅷 **Pousada de Salceda** (🛏8, €12/40/47): 🍴🆆🅳📶, N-547 km 75, ☎981502767 ✉, 🕐all year, +400m to the left

27.6 Brea 🅰 🅷 🍴🚌

🅰 **El Chalet** (🛏12, €12/-/40): 🍴🆆🅳📶, A Brea 5, ☎659380723 ✉, 🕐Apr-Oct, closed weekends
🅷 **O Mesón** (€32/44): 🍴🆆🅳📶, A Brea 16, ☎981511040 ✉
🅷 **The Way** (€20/34/42): 🆆🅳📶, A Brea 36, ☎628120202 ✉

30.4 Santa Irene A H 🅿️

Santa Irene has a small 18th-century chapel dedicated to Saint Irene, which has a Baroque retablo and a covered fountain with a 1692 image of the saint. Saint Irene was a Portuguese martyr from the 7th century.

A Xunta (⛺36, €6): 🔣, ☎660396825, 🕐1pm a.y., no cookware, restaurant +1.5 km
A Santa Irene (⛺15, €13): 🔣, ☎981511000, 🕐Apr-Oct, charming
A Astrar (⛺24, €10-13): 🔣, Astrar 18, ☎608092820 📝, 🕐Mar-Nov, +700m

32.0 A Rúa H 🍴 🅿️

H Casa O Acivro (€38/48): 🍴, A Rúa 28, ☎981511316 📝
H Hotel O Pino (€38/50): 🍴, A Rúa 9, ☎981511035 📝, +200m

33.0 Arca A H 🍴 🛒 ⛪ ➕ ℹ️ 🅿️

Also O Pino or O Pedrouzo, ℹ️ ☎638612496, 🕐12-6pm daily in summer, 🛒 Deportes Remanso, c/Pedrouzo 11, ☎981511380

At the entrance to Arca, turn L to enter town for accommodations or services, or continue straight to bypass Arca, passing one café on the far side of town (saves 0.6km). Arca once housed the Hospital de Santa Eulalia de Arca and the Capilla de San Antón de Arca, though nothing remains of them today. There is a modern Iglesia de Santa Eulalia de Arca and impressive oak trees near town hall.

1. **A Xunta** (⛺120, €6): 🔣, Lugo 30, ☎660396826, 🕐1pm all year, behind post office
2. **A H O Burgo** (⛺10, €10/28/38): 🔣, Lugo 47, ☎630404138 📝, 🕐Apr-Oct
3. **A Porta Santiago** (⛺54, €10): 🔣, Lugo 11, ☎981511103 📝, 🕐Mar-Nov
4. **A O Trisquel** (⛺68, €10-12): 🔣, Picón 1, ☎616644740 📝
5. **A Otero** (⛺36, €10): 🔣, Forcarei 2, ☎671663374 📝, 🕐Apr-Oct
6. **A Edreira** (⛺56, €10-12): 🔣, Fonte 19, ☎981511365 📝, 🕐Mar-Oct
7. **A REM** (⛺50, €10-12): 🔣, Iglesia 7, ☎981510407, 🕐all year
8. **A Cruceiro Pedrouzo** (⛺94, €10-12): 🔣, Iglesia 7, ☎981511371, 🕐Mar-Nov
9. **H Pensión Compas** (€25/35): 🍴, Lugo 47, ☎981511309 📝
10. **H Pensión Platas** (€40/55): 📶, Lugo 26, ☎981511378 📝
11. **H Una Estrella Dorada** (€28/39): 🔣, Lugo 10, ☎630018363
12. **H Pensión Pedrouzo** (€25/35): 🔣, Santiago 13, ☎671663375 📝
13. **H Pensión Arca** (€30/50): 🔣, Mollados 25, ☎657888594 📝
14. **H Pensión Maribel** (€40/50): 🔣, Mollados 23, ☎981511404 📝
15. **H Pensión Avenida** (€29/39): 📶, Santiago 23, ☎698147113 📝
16. **H Pensión Maruja** (€20/30): 🍴, Nova 9, ☎981511406 📝

13 ARCA TO SANTIAGO

20.0km (12.4mi), ⏱ 5.5-7 Hours, Difficulty: ▬☐☐
🅿 83%, 21.2km, Ⓤ 17%, 4.4km

💡 The path today passes through more eucalyptus forests and several small villages to arrive at Monte do Gozo, within sight (on a clear day) of Santiago's cathedral spires. The last 5km are city walking. The atmosphere entering Santiago is often jubilant, with singing, shouting and congratulations, no matter how dreary the weather. Leave early to arrive in time for the noon pilgrim mass.

3.4 Amenal
- **Amenal** (€60): Amenal 12, ☏981510431

10.0 Lavacolla — "place of washing"
- **Lavacolla** (🛏34, €12): Lavacolla 35, ☏981897274
- **A Concho** (€30-35/35-45): Lavacolla 1, ☏981888390
- **Casa Lavacolla** (€40-60): Lavacolla 20, ☏659881868
- **San Paio** (€38/49): ☏981-888205
- **Garcas** (€35/50): Naval 2, ☏981888225
- **Ruta Jacobea** (€69): Lavacolla 41, ☏981888211
- **Pazo Xan Xordo** (€65): Xan Xordo 6, ☏981888259, +900m

14.6 San Marcos
- **Akelarre** (€35-45/40-50): San Marcos 37B, ☏981552689

15.1 Monte do Gozo — Galician: *Monxoi* "Mount Joy"
- **Xunta** (🛏500, €6): ☏981558942, ⏱1pm all year, rooms of 8, bunker-like
- **Monte do Gozo (Polskie)** (par, 🛏40, don): Rúa das Estelas, ☏981597222, ⏱May-Oct, run by Polish volunteers
- **Santiago Apóstal** (€50-70): San Marcos 1, ☏981557155

20.0 Santiago de Compostela
See city map and accommodations list on p. 62-63.

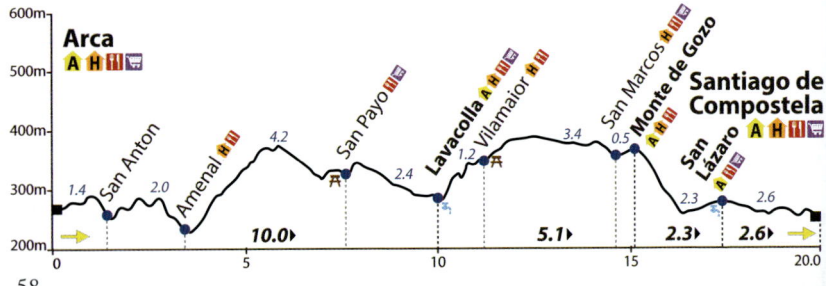

Arca
0.0
San Antón
1.4
Amenal
3.4
Cimadevila
Castrofeito
Santiso
N-634
N-547
Alvarín
Vilachá
Pereira
Santiago (Lavacolla)
San Payo
7.6
San Pelayo
Lavacolla
10.0
Benaval
San Roque
Frades
A Enfesta
A-54
AP-9
Reboredo
11.2
Vilamaior
TV Galicia
Camping San Marcos
San Marcos
14.6
15.1
Marcos
Monte do Gozo
Bando
San Lázaro
17.4
San Lázaro
Santiago de Compostela
20.0
Cathedral
Loureda
A Moa
Caneda
Zaramacedo
A Cacharela
Outeiro
N
2 km
0
1
2

Santiago de Compostela

- Meiga Backpackers **10**
- Basquinos 45 **11**
- Carme †
- † Santa Clara
- **12** La Salle
- Parque de Domingos Bonaval
- San Francisco †
- Altaïr **24**
- O Fogar de Teodomiro
- 🏛 Arte
- **25** Costa Vella
- **13 14** Linares
- Pilgrim Office ℹ
- Domingo †
- Blanco **19**
- A Casa do Peregrino
- Po Ga
- Santiago KM-0 **18**
- San Martín Pinario **26**
- **15** Plaza Cervantes
- Casa Reis
- Dos Reis **27**
- **17** Azabache
- **16** Last Stamp
- **28** Costa Azul
- Hortas
- Police
- Praza do Obradoiro
- Cathedral † San Paio
- **20** Roots and Boots
- Poza de Bar
- Pombal
- Fonseca **29**
- 🏛 Pilgrimage
- Mundoalbergue ✉
- ℹ Tourist Info (Galicia)
- Seminario Menor **9**
- **21**
- Parque Alameda
- † Susana
- Villar
- ℹ Tourist Info (Santiago)
- **30** Suso
- Vixe da Cerca
- Parque Belvis
- Senra
- **31** Centro
- Xoan Carlos I
- To Finisterre and Muxia
- Galeiras
- Dos Rodo
- Compostela **23**
- Praza Roxa
- Salvador
- Arxentina
- La Estación **22**
- Ferrol
- Vilagracia
- Romero Donallo

17.4 San Lázaro/outer Santiago A 🍴🛒🚌

1. **A** **Xunta** (📞80, €10 first night, €7 for 2nd/3rd): 🐾 W D, San Lázaro, ☎981571488, 🕐all year
2. **A** **Fin del Camino** (assoc, 📞110, €9): 🐾 W D 🍴 📶, Moscova, ☎981587324, 🕐May-Oct
3. **A** **Santo Santiago** (📞40, €10-12): 🐾 W D 🍴 📶, Lázaro Valiño 3, ☎657402403, 🕐all year
4. **A** **Acuario** (📞70, €13-20): 🐾 W D 🍴 📶 Ⓞ, Estocolmo 2, ☎981575438, 🕐Mar-Nov
5. **A** **Monterrey** (📞36, €12-15): 🐾 W D 📶, Fontiñas 65, ☎655484299, 🕐all year
6. **A** **La Credential** (📞36, €10-14): 🐾 W D 🍴 📶 Ⓞ, Fonte Concheiros 13, ☎981068083, 🕐Mar-Nov
7. **A** **La Estrella de Santiago** (📞24, €10-16): 🐾 W 📶, Concheiros 36-38, ☎881973926, 🕐all year

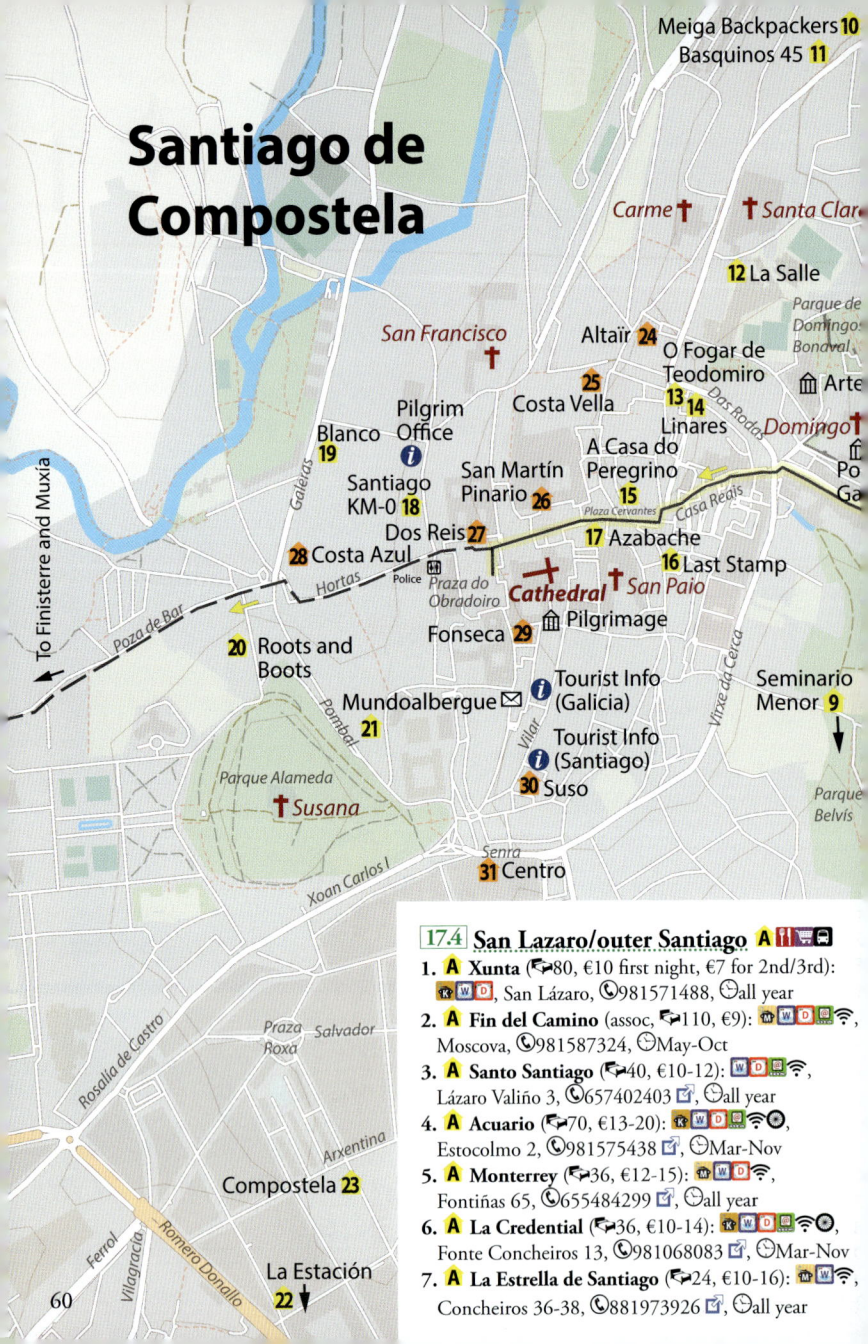

60

0.0 Santiago de Compostela 🅰 🅗 🍴🛒⛾⊕⊙ℹ🚌✈

- **Santiago city**: Rúa do Vilar 63, ☎981-555129 ✉, ⊙Daily 9am-9pm (summer)
- **Galicia**: Rúa do Vilar 30, ☎902-332010 ✉, ⊙M-F 10am-8pm, Sa 11am-2pm, 5-7pm, Su 11am-2pm
- **Pilgrim office**: Rúa Carretas 33, ☎981-568846 ✉, ⊙Daily M-Sa 9am-9pm (summer), left luggage, ♿

- 🅐 **Porta Real** (⛺24, €10-20): 🛁🅦🅳🍴🛜, Concheiros 10, ☎633610114 ✉, ⊙all year
- 🅐🅗 **Seminario Menor** (⛺177, €11-15/14-20/28-40): 🛁🅦🅳🍴🛜, Quiroga Palacios 2, ☎881031768 ✉, ⊙Mar-Oct, all beds not bunks, some reports of theft, lockers available
- 0. 🅐 **Meiga Backpackers** (hostel, ⛺30, €13-15): 🛁🅦🅳🍴🛜, Basquiños 67, ☎981570846 ✉, ⊙a. y.
- 1. 🅐 **Basquinos 45** (⛺10, €10-16): 🅦🅳🛜, Basquiños 45, ☎661894536 ✉, ⊙all year
- 2. 🅐🅗 **La Salle** (⛺20, €17-20/37/59): 🛁🅦🅳🍴🛜⊙, Tras Santa Clara, ☎682158011 ✉
- 3. 🅐 **Fogar Teodomiro** (⛺20, €13-18): 🛁🅦🅳🍴🛜, Algalia Arriba 3, ☎981582920 ✉, ⊙10am all year
- 4. 🅐🅗 **Linares** (⛺14, €22/60/70): 🛁🅦🅳🛜, Algalia Abajo 34, ☎981580443 ✉
- 5. 🅐🅗 **A Casa Do Peregrino** (€15-25/65/80): 🛜, Azabacheria 2, ☎981573931 ✉
- 6. 🅐 **Last Stamp** (⛺54, €18-25): 🛁🅦🅳🍴🛜, Preguntoiro 10, ☎981563525 ✉, ⊙mid Jan.-mid Dec
- 7. 🅐 **Azabache** (⛺20, €14-18): 🛁🅦🅳🛜, Azabachería 15, ☎981071254 ✉, ⊙all year
- 8. 🅐 **Santiago KM-0** (⛺41, €20-25): 🛁🍴🅦🅳🛜, das Carretas 11, ☎881974992 ✉
- 9. 🅐🅗 **Blanco** (⛺20, €20/-/40): 🛁🛜, Galeras 30, ☎881976850 ✉
- 0. 🅐 **Roots and Boots** (hstl., ⛺48, €16-21): 🛁🅦🅳🍴🛜, Campo Cruceiro do Galo 7, ☎699631594 ✉
- 1. 🅐 **Mundoalbergue** (⛺34, €16-18): 🛁🅦🅳🍴🛜, San Clemente 26, ☎981588625 ✉, ⊙all year
- 2. 🅐🅗 **La Estación** (⛺24, €15/30/40): 🅦🅳🛜⊙, Xoana Nogueira 14, ☎981594624 ✉, ⊙all year
- 3. 🅐 **Compostela** (⛺36, €16-18): 🛁🅦🅳🍴🛜, San Pedro de Mezonzo 28, ☎881017840 ✉
- 4. 🅗 **Altaïr Hotel** (€87/120): 🍴🛜, Loureiros 12, ☎981554712 ✉
- 5. 🅗 **Costa Vella** (€60/83): 🍴🛜, Porta da Pena 17, ☎981569530 ✉, restored Jesuit house
- 6. 🅗⭐ **San Martín Pinario** (pilgrim €25/40 🍴): 🍴🛜, Plaza Inmaculada 3, ☎981560282 ✉
- 7. 🅗 **Dos Reis Católicos** (€200+/240+): Praza do Obradoiro, ☎981582200 ✉, Parador
- 8. 🅗 **Costa Azul** (€22-40/30-60): 🛜, Das Galeras 18, ☎602451906 ✉
- 9. 🅗 **Pensión Fonseca** (€40/60): 🛜, Fonseca 1, ☎981584145 ✉
- 0. 🅗 **Hostal Suso** (€58-70): 🍴🛜, Villar 65, ☎981586611 ✉
- 1. 🅗 **Pensión Centro** (€30-40/40-50): 🛜, Senra 11, ☎981588465

Spanish Phrasebook

Local Languages: The main language you'll hear on the Camino is Spanish, though each region has at least one other official language, such as Galician in Galicia. Many local people along the Camino do not speak English. Learning some phrases in Spanish will greatly enhance your experience and reflects a respect for local culture that is often much appreciated. But don't let not speaking Spanish deter you from the Camino. Below is a very basic phrase list; a more comprehensive phrasebook is available on our website.

Greetings and Small Talk
Hello - *hola*
Goodbye/see you later - *adiós/hasta luego*
Good morning - *buenos días*
Good afternoon/evening - *buenas tardes*
Good night - *buenas noches*
Yes/no/maybe - *sí/no/quizás*
Please - *por favor*
How are you? - *¿Cómo estás?*
I am fine. - *Estoy bien.*
Where are you from? - *¿De dónde eres?*
I'm from... - *Soy de...*
  The USA - *Los Estados Unidos*
  Canada - *Canadá*
  England - *Inglaterra*
  Ireland - *Irlanda*
  Australia - *Australia*
  South Africa - *Sudáfrica*
Thank you - *gracias*
You're welcome - *de nada*
Excuse me - *disculpa*
Nice to meet you. - *Mucho gusto.*
I (don't) understand/Do you understand? - *(No) Entiendo/¿Entiendes?*
Do you speak English? - *¿Habla Inglés?*
I don't speak Spanish - *No hablo Español*
Please speak more slowly. - *Por favor, hable más despacio.*
One minute, please. - *Un momento, por favor.*
Walk well/happy trails - *Buen camino!*

What time does it open/close? - *¿A qué hora abre/cierra?*
Where is (are) the...? - *¿Donde está(n) …?*
  bathroom - *los servicios*
  hospital - *el hospital*
  a hostel – *un albergue*
Where can I find water? - *¿Dónde puedo encontrar agua?*
Do you have wifi? - *¿Tiene wifi? (wee-fee)*
Password - *contraseña, clave*

Problems - *problemas*
I'm lost. - *Estoy perdido.*
Help! - *Ayúdame!/Socorro!*
Call the police! - *Llama a la policía!*
Call a doctor! - *Llama a un médico!*
I need a doctor/dentist. - *Necesito un doctor/un dentista*
Go away! - *Véte!*
Leave me alone! - *Déjame en paz!*
Medicine - *medicamentos*
Pharmacy - *farmacia*
Medical center/clinic - *centro de salud*
Blister - *ampolla*
Fracture/sprain - *fractura*
I'm sick. - *Estoy enfermo/a...*
I'm allergic to - *Tengo alergia a...*
Penicillin - *la penicilina*
Bee sting - *picadura de abeja*
Beg bugs - *los chinches*
Pain - *dolor*

Notes

About the Authors

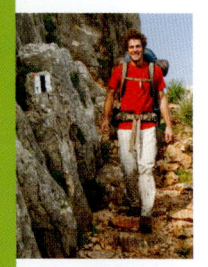

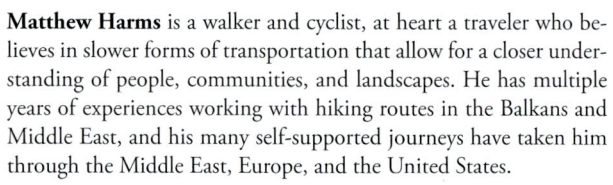

Matthew Harms is a walker and cyclist, at heart a traveler who believes in slower forms of transportation that allow for a closer understanding of people, communities, and landscapes. He has multiple years of experiences working with hiking routes in the Balkans and Middle East, and his many self-supported journeys have taken him through the Middle East, Europe, and the United States.

Anna Dintaman and **David Landis** are the cofounders of Village to Village Press, LLC and bring over 10 years of experience working with walking routes in the Mediterranean and Middle East. Both avid hikers and cyclists, their experience ranges from backpacking Patagonia and Nepal to hiking in the Alps, Andes, and Appalachian mountains to cycling across the United States. They have shared a deep love of the Camino since their first journeys on the Francés route in 2009. In 2007, David cofounded the Jesus Trail, a hiking trail that connects sites from the life of Jesus. They enjoy introducing their children to the joys of walking, the outdoors, and learning from other cultures.

Feedback, comments & corrections welcomed: info@caminoguidebook.com

- facebook.com/caminoguidebooks
- instagram.com/caminoguidebook
- twitter.com/caminoguidebook
- pinterest.com/caminoguidebook

Village to Village Press, LLC specializes in publishing hiking guidebooks and supporting trail development projects, especially with an emphasis on pilgrimage along the Camino de Santiago and in the Middle East and Mediterranean regions.

CaminoGuidebook.com
Visit for free planning information including maps, GPS tracks and frequently asked questions.

CaminoCyclist.com
Your portal to biking the Camino!

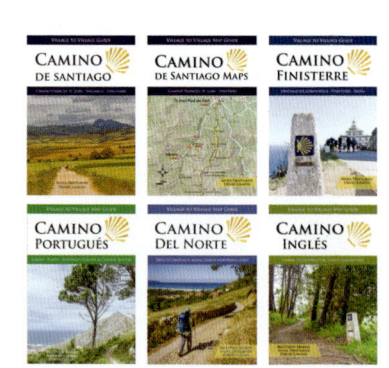

VILLAGE TO VILLAGE PRESS
WWW.VILLAGETOVILLAGEPRESS.COM